UNIX IN EASY STEPS

MOHAMMED AZAM
Director, Synergy Software Group
Madras

PUBLISHING FOR ONE WORLD

NEW AGE INTERNATIONAL (P) LIMITED, PUBLISHERS
New Delhi • Bangalore • Chennai • Cochin • Guwahati • Hyderabad
Jalandhar • Kolkata • Lucknow • Mumbai • Ranchi
Visit us at **www.newagepublishers.com**

Published by New Age International (P) Ltd., Publishers
First Edition : 1993
Reprint : 2012

BRANCHES

- **Bangalore** 37/10, 8th Cross (Near Hanuman Temple), Azad Nagar, Chamarajpet Bangalore-560 018. Tel.: (080) 26756823, Telefax: 26756820 E-mail: bangalore@newagepublishers.com
- **Chennai** 26, Damodaran Street, T. Nagar, Chennai-600 017 Tel.: (044) 24353401, Telefax: 24351463 E-mail: chennai@newagepublishers.com
- **Cochin** CC-39/1016, Carrier Station Road, Ernakulam South, Cochin-682 016 Tel.: (0484) 2377004, Telefax: 4051303 E-mail: cochin@newagepublishers.com
- **Guwahati** Hemsen Complex, Mohd. Shah Road, Paltan Bazar, Near Starline Hotel Guwahati-781 008. Tel.: (0361) 2513881, Telefax: 2543669 E-mail: guwahati@newagepublishers.com
- **Hyderabad** 105, 1st Floor, Madhiray Kaveri Tower, 3-2-19, Azam Jahi Road, Nimboliadda Hyderabad-500 027. Tel.: (040) 24652456, Telefax: 24652457 E-mail: hyderabad@newagepublishers.com
- **Kolkata** RDB Chambers (Formerly Lotus Cinema) 106A, 1st Floor, S.N. Banerjee Road, Kolkata-700 014. Tel.: (033) 22273773, Telefax: 22275247 E-mail: kolkata@newagepublishers.com
- **Lucknow** 16-A, Jopling Road, Lucknow-226 001 Tel.: (0522) 2209578, 4045297,Telefax: 2204098 E-mail: lucknow@newagepublishers.com
- **Mumbai** 142C, Victor House, Ground Floor, N.M. Joshi Marg, Lower Parel Mumbai- 400 013. Tel.: (022) 24927869, Telefax: 24915415 E-mail: mumbai@newagepublishers.com
- **New Delhi** 22, Golden House, Daryaganj, New Delhi-110 002 Tel.: (011) 23262368, 23262370, Telefax: 43551305 E-mail: sales@newagepublishers.com

ISBN (10) : 81-224-0552-5
ISBN (13) : 978-81-224-0552-1

₹ 175.00

C-12-08-6462

Printed in India at Ajit Printers, Delhi.

PUBLISHING FOR ONE WORLD
NEW AGE INTERNATIONAL (P) LIMITED, PUBLISHERS
7/30 A, Daryaganj, New Delhi-110002
Visit us at **www.newagepublishers.com**

To my parents and my brother Mohammed Siraj

FOREWORD

UNIX has become the 'Open Sesame' for all aspirants for a career in computers. Interestingly, the creators of UNIX themselves are quite surprised that what they put together as a special purpose operating system for a workstation, has become an industry standard. It was meant to help a scientist/engineer to put together a more complex program by being able to make the output of one module serve as input to another, and also have a convenient directory structure. Actually, creators of UNIX wanted to have a convenient workstation for producing technical paper and documents. That is why even a bare minimum UNIX has the very nice editor 'vi'. UNIX has still many problems to be ironed out before it can be a good general purpose operating system for transaction processing in today's networking approach to computing. One may wonder how it has become an industry standard with all the drawbacks, which are however being slowly eliminated. Case of UNIX illustrates how standards come about - not because one has a perfect example, but wide spread use makes it a de-facto standard which sooner or later becomes a standard. Perhaps, this is the only case where having chosen a standard one is modifying/extending to make it fit the role. Sri Mohammed Azam has tried to make it easy for beginners to learn UNIX effectively. Delightful figures and the chatty style of making the reader learn by doing is very necessary for readers who do not have extensive experience in programming. For Sri Azam this book is a labour of love for he had no hesitation to revise extensively every time he got a good suggestion to make the book better for self study. UNIX is big and getting bigger and anybody who masters what is given in this book will certainly have confidence to tackle the real UNIX manuals. Inspite of the fact that this book is very nice to read one cannot learn UNIX, in the sense of coming to terms with UNIX, unless one gets down to do all the exercises, particularly the real-life exercises given in the end of the book.

UNIX has prevailed in that even IBM has accepted it. If literacy in computers is soon going to mean knowing UNIX, Sri Azam should be thanked for making UNIX easy.

H.N. MAHABALA
IIT MADRAS

PREFACE

In learning any subject, the first steps are the most crucial. The subject should be properly introduced in order to hold the student's interest. The student then understands and appreciates the subject better. This is more so in the case of Computer languages in general. They tend to be very cryptic and the vast documentation that accompany them can blunt the enthusiasm of even a very keen learner.

The goal of this book is to help a student learn UNIX in easy stages. UNIX is a very vast subject and this book does not attempt to cover all of it. Only the most frequently used commands are covered. Extra effort has been made to make this book easy to read and digest even for a casual reader. All the commands and concepts are explained with examples. At the end of each chapter a number of questions are put to the student. The student is expected to attempt these questions without refering to the material. This will give a feedback to the student as to how well and how much of the concepts and commands have been understood.

You can get the best out of this book if you sit before an UNIX terminal and attempt the examples given. If an UNIX terminal is not readily available you can still go through the material to get an idea of how the UNIX system functions.This book is meant for beginners as well as experienced users. Advanced utilities have been discussed which the experienced user will find interesting.

Finally we have Fast Track which is a listing of the various commands covered in this book. The beginner as well as the Unix veterans will find it an useful source for reference.

I believe that learning Unix can be fun and stimulating. Have Fun!

ACKNOWLEDGEMENTS

This book would not have been possible without the help of many kind souls. The people at Klass Computers were of immense help. Special thanks to S.Mohan the propreitor of Klass Computers and R.Mythili. Prof. H.N.Mahabala of IIT Madras was kind enough to offer suggestions to improve this book and finally crowned the effort with a foreword. N.Mohan of Sundaram Finance and Mohan Bangaruswamy of Wipro lent a lot of their time to go through the material and offer their comments and suggestions. Prof. Robert Charles went through the material and ironed out the wrinkles in my prose and Gayathri Kotapalli deserves special mention for helping out with the proof reading. Mr S. Padmanabhan of Padmaja for his encouragement. Last but not the least Ajit Kumar of Mahabeer who helped me with his contacts and Mr Govindan and Mr Puroshattaman of Wiley Eastern who were kind enough to encourage a budding author. And above all I thank the Almighty for giving me the strength to take up such a task.

Mohammed Azam

CONTENTS

1

THE OPERATING SYSTEM

If you were to call on a wealthy friend of yours, invariably the door would be opened by a housekeeper. The housekeeper would show you in, and ask you to wait in the drawing room. (Assuming of course that you are suitably dressed and do not look like a person with doubtful intentions). If you ask for a glass of water or sherry (depending upon the local custom) it would be provided. Your friend comes in, you trade news and in the process you observe that the housekeeper is incharge of all the housekeeping activities. Some of them done by him personally and some delegated to the other staff in the household. However all the interaction is done through the housekeeper.

Enough of this housekeeper business. You are wondering why we have to talk of a housekeeper when we are supposed to be talking about the UNIX operating system.

The purpose of introducing a housekeeper was to provide you an analogy. This is how it goes.

(1) When you switch on your UNIX system a message comes on, asking you to login (i.e.) to enter your name & password. Just as you hand in your visiting card.

(2) After you have entered your password the UNIX system checks it internally to see if it is correct. Again, the housekeeper would verify your name etc., from the appointment book to see if it matched. If so you are permitted in.

Just as the housekeeper takes care of the household chores and responds to your requests/commands, the operating system also takes care of housekeeping activities in the computer system. This includes maintenance of files, allocation of resource etc. We will discuss in brief about the functions of the operating system once you are introduced to some of the usual terms used in computer parlance. It is not enough if you have money in your pocket when you go to a hotel. You should also be able to order the right dish so that you eat exactly what you want. So is the case with other things, including computers. You have to know what each term means so that you do not get mixed up. Right?

1.1

Operating System The software interface between the user and the computer.

1.2

M.S.Dos Supplied The acronym for Microsoft Disk Operating System. An Operating System (OS) developed by Microsoft, which is usually supplied on floppy disks. This is an example of the 'SINGLE USER' Operating System which means that only one user can use the computer at a time.

1.3

Multiuser operating system An operating system like the UNIX which allows several users to work on the system at the same time.

1.4

Commands Word(s)/characters typed on the terminal which instruct 'command' the computer to do a particular task.

1.5

Prompt A character displayed on the left hand side of the screen to tell the user that the system is ready for the next command. It 'prompts' the user to enter the next command. The prompt can be a '$', or '%', or A etc.

1.6

Files A collection of records just like the file that we maintain about clients or suppliers etc.

1.7

C.P.U The Central Processing Unit is the unit which does all the processing of data. Processing can be computation, comparison, file updation etc.

1.8

Memory The place where all the processing is done. The memory is measured in bytes.

1024 bytes = 1 kilobyte or 1 kb
1000 kb = 1 megabyte or 1 mb

Program A set of instructions in a logical sequence which instructs the computer, as to how a particular function (processing) has to be done.

The Operating System is a group of programs where each program performs a specific task. The number of programs & tasks are many. In this chapter we will only look at the functions with a bird's eye view.

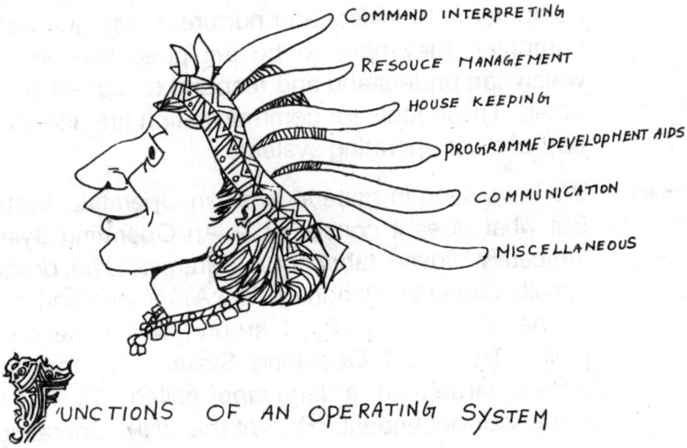

1.1 The Operating System

1.9

Resource Management An important function of the Operating System is management of resources like C.P.U. time, allocation of printers, Hard disks to users. It permits or restricts access to data depending upon the user. As you go through the subsequent chapters you will know how this is done.

1.10

Command Interpretting It invokes the relevant routines depending upon the command typed by the user. It checks for the correct syntax, and the user's authority to use the particular command before invoking the relevant/programs that will execute the command.

1.11

Housekeeping It manages the files/data stored and accessed by the user. It discards unused files, repairs damaged/corrupted files and ensures that the user can work in a clean environment (An ideal housekeeper !).

1.12

Program Development Aids In order to meet day to day data processing needs, one has to write the code, correct it and convert it into a form that the computer can understand. You need editors, debugging tools and compilers. These are also provided by the operating system.

1.13

Communication Computers, like men believe in socialising! But if one computer is to initiate and nurture a dialogue with another computer, they have to be equipped with an interpreter which can understand and respond to signals sent by each other. These tools for communication are also provided as part of most operating systems.

Unix vs Others We have seen in general what an Operating System does. But what does it consist of ? An Operating System is an intricately woven fabric of programs. The programs are usually coded in a language like Assembler and are specific to the processor [C.P.U.] around which the computer is built. The UNIX Operating System, on the contrary is written largely in a language called 'C' which is not processor dependent. Part of the UNIX Operating System code is however written on Assembler. This means that UNIX is highly portable (i.e) it can run on various processors (C.P.U's) with little modification. Other advantages of UNIX will be covered in subsequent chapters.

2

STRUCTURE OF UNIX

In the last chapter we saw what an operating system does, ie. its functions. In this chapter we shall see the way the Unix Operating System is structured and how this structural difference makes it a better Operating System compared to the other conventional Operating Systems offered.

The responsibilities of an Operating System are command interpretation, I/O control, communications etc.,etc,. To perform these tasks a large number of complicated as well as simple programs are needed. These programs can be independent or otherwise. Traditionally all these programs would be put together forming one large program. Hence the Operating System becomes a large program and occupies a large amount of memory space. As a result the system response was very slow. Then along came UNIX with a fresh structure for an Operating System.

The UNIX Operating System can be divided into three parts structurally. Following is the structure.

A core unit which will interact with the hardware for low-level functions.

An outer unit which will interact with the user to perform functions desired by the user. The functions can be computer related or otherwise.

The file system

The idea was to keep the units related but still separate so that the entire program did not park itself in the memory and slow down the system. Let us now examine the three units one by one.

kernel The core unit is called the kernel. The kernel's task include C.P.U. scheduling, allocating the necesssary hardware, controlling I/O operations etc. How it allots the C.P.U. to various processess is very interesting. (A process is a running program). Unix, as we know is a multi-user, multi-tasking Operating System, which means that several users can work on the system at the same time and each user can submit several jobs for execution at the same time. Now, since there are several jobs submitted and running simultaneously, the kernel has to give them a tag or an identification. The simplest form of identification for the kernel is an integer. So, for every job that is initiated the kernel assigns an identification number called P.I.D (Process I.D). The kernel maintains a table called "Process Tab" which describes every running process. When a process is initiated the kernel creates an entry in the process table and discards the entry when the process is completed/halted.

It is said "Seeing, is believing". But not so always. We see that the UNIX system is able to respond to so many users simultaneously, which means that it can do several jobs at once. But this is not so in reality. Let us take a peek iniside to see what exactly is happening. When several users initiate several jobs at the same time the scene inside will be very much like the scene when somebody has announced that he would distribute Rs.100 to anybody who can say "I LOVE UNIX" (the number of notes are limited! HURRY!!). Every body would like to be heard first so that he does not miss the money. So is the case with processes. But remember, the kernel has kept track of every process initiated/running. The entry of each process in the Process Table also indicates the process priority. THE PROCESS PRIORITY IS A MEASURE OF THE IMPORTANCE OF THE PROCESS (One begins to think of VIPs and VVIPs !). The kernel refers to the priority of the processes when alloting the CPU to it. Once the CPU is alloted to a job it will run for an interval and then the CPU will be alloted to another job (Why this interval business?). An interval is a small amount of time for which a process runs. This ensures that all the processes get a chance to run. A process can be halted for any of the following reasons.

- The process exhausts its interval.
- The process can go no further.

- The process has to wait for an event to occur.
- Another process has assumed higher priority and the CPU is alloted to this new process.

The allocation/reallocation is done at a mind boggling speed and the users all along think that the system is responding to all of them simultaneously.

swapping

Just as the CPU time is a valuable resource so is the memory space. As always, a valuable resource has too many users and too little of it is available. Memory space as you know is used by the Operating System, by the program and the data which has to be processed. With a number of users working on the system, at any point of time the memory space available will be less than the space required. The Kernel cannot shout "I WANT MORE MEMORY OR I WILL NOT BE ABLE TO WORK !!" nor can it tell the user "THE MEMORY IS FULL TODAY, TRY YOUR LUCK TOMORROW !". A good Operating System should be able to handle it all. And this is what happens: If a process has to be executed all parts of the process have to be in the memory. Now if one process is running then the other process need not be present in the memory (Logical!). The kernel therefore moves the waiting process to the secondary storage (ie) the hard disk, thereby the currently running process has all the memory space needed. This is called swapping. This process too takes place at a dazzling speed.

context switching

The Kernel does its work in two modes. One is the user mode and the other is the Kernel mode. The two modes are otherwise known as UNRESTRICTED MODE and RESTRICTED MODE respectively. When the Kernel is processing a program it is working in the user mode. If in the program there is a need to create a file then the Kernel switches to the kernel mode to do the file creation. Once this is done the Kernel automatically switches its context to the user mode to execute the next statement. This is called context switching.

an illustration

The UNIX Operating System consists of a large number of small individual programs which are invoked & loaded into the memory only when required. A case in point is the 'LOG IN' process. When you switch on the system you see a message prompting you to enter your **login name**. You enter your name and your password **(if necessary)** and bingo ! you are on ! Sounds very simple from the outside. Let's take a look at the internals of the LOGIN process.

When you "power on" the system, the firmware loads the **"/unix"** file in the memory and executes it. The **"/unix"** file contains the kernel which sets up the necessary processes to let you log in.

kernel First a process table is created. The kernel itself being the first process gets a PID 0. The kernel process ends only when the system is halted.

init Secondly the kernel invokes the **'init'** process by executing the **/etc/init** file. This process is responsible for the initiation of all other process. It has a PID 1 and halts only when the system is halted. But unlike the kernel it does not interact with the hardware and is fully dependent on the kernel for all such interactions.

inittab Once the **'init'** process is on, it in turn invokes the **/etc/inittab** file. The **inittab** file informs**'init'**, as to which terminal can be used & which terminal is ready and in a position to accept the login message. EXIT **'inittab'**. ENTER **'getty'**.

getty The ball is now back in **'init's** court. **'init'** then invokes the **/etc/getty**. This file has the various parameters for communication between the terminal and the computer. Using these parameters the login prompt is displayed.

login When you enter your log-in name the **/login** program takes over. If you have a password for your account the **/login** program prompts you to enter your password. Once you enter your password (the correct password) it will inform you that you have successfully logged in. There you are. You can wipe the sweat from the tired brow! Ha!

conclusion The above explanation was to illustrate how the UNIX system works using the software programs as tools rather than including them in the main body of the Operating System. Each program was invoked when necessary and discarded when the required function was completed.

We will now talk about the outer unit which interacts with the user. The Public Relations Officer (PRO) of your organisation or any PRO for that matter will be a person with a lot of polish. He will not get upset even if you shout at him (it does not mean that you shout at any PRO you come across). He will convey all your heartache to his management omitting any unparliamentary language you may have used to garnish your message. And what transpires between the management and the PRO you do not know but you get the reply to whatever you wanted from the management. Well goodbye PRO welcome SHELL !

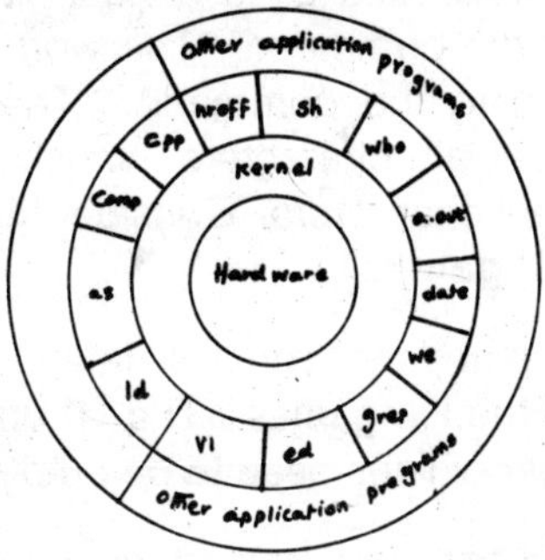

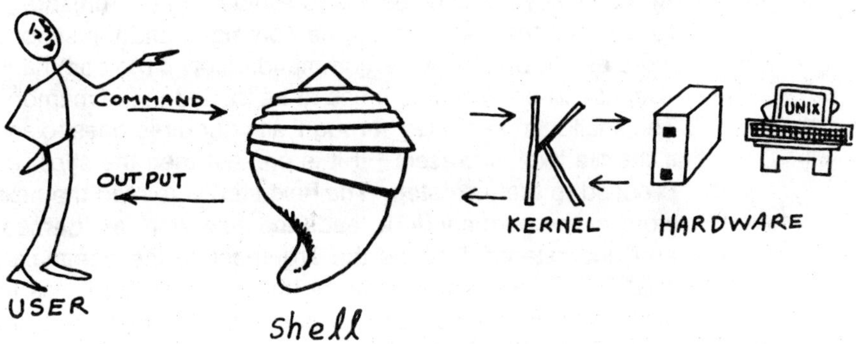

Structure of Unix

shell

The outer unit which interacts with the user is called shell. (It is an apt name too!). The shell acts like an interpreter between you and the kernel. The commands that you type are interpreted by the shell and passed on to the kernel for execution. The result, if any, is output by the shell in a form the user can understand.

Presently there are several shells available (not sea shells !) on the UNIX Operating System. Some of these are the Bourne Shell, 'C' Shell, the Korn Shell, etc. The most popular of the shells are the Bourne and the 'C' shell. We will be discussing only the Bourne Shell in this book. The chapter on shell programming deals with the functions of the shell in detail. In this chapter we will limit our discussions with the way the shell interprets a command.

The shell follows some basic rules which are as follows:

The first 'word' (A word is a set of character(s) ending with a space) is interpreted as the command. If the second word is preceeded by a minus(-) then it is treated as an option of the command. The words following this are the arguments to the command. The shell also recognises some special characters which will be covered in subsequent characters. Consider the following:

{wc -l games}

This command as you will later learn performs a word count on the file games. The '-l' option specifies that only the number of lines need to be output.

At the end of the command when you press the ENTER or RETURN key the shell begins to evaluate the command. It recognises the first word as the command and the second word as the option to the command. Now if the command **'wc'** has to be executed it has to be loaded in the memory. The shell then searches 'through' all your directories to see if the file **'wc'** is present. If it is present then the shell will proceed to the next step. The next step is to read the next word of the command. It reads the next word as **'games'** and understands it to be the argument to the command. That is **'games'** is the name of the file on which it has to act. Now it will search the directory in which you are working to see if the file **'games'** is available. If it is available it will pass the command, the option and the arguments to the kernel for execution. In case the file **'wc'** is not found it will display a message **"wc not found"**. If the file **'games'** is not found it will display a message **"file not found"**. After the execution the shell passes on the output given by the kernel to the user in a form the user can understand. More about shell later. Some of the utilities and their functions are described in Table IIA.

COMMAND SUMMARY

UTILITY	FUNCTION
ls	directory listing
rm	remove file
cp	copy a file
mv	rename a file
mkdir	Make new directory
rmdir	remove directory
pwd	print working directory
chmod	change file attributes
chgrp	change group
chown	change owner
mkfs	make file system
mount/umount	mount/unmount file system
date	display system date
cal	display calendar
sort	sort a file
awk	pattern matching
cat	display or concatenate files
pg	display pagewise
man	online help
find	locate a file

TABLE IIA

The Unix Tree

Let us take a look at the file system in UNIX. One very important feature of the UNIX system is the treatment of devices as files. All the devices are addressed as files. For example if you wanted to take a print out of a file, the system would simply write the file to the printer device file just as you write to any other file. This lets you very effectively control the access to any device. More about security later.

The Unix system recognizes the following types of files:

(1) Ordinary files
(2) Directory files
(3) Special or device files
(4) FIFO files

How are these files arranged/laid out in the Unix File System. Most books compare the Unix File System to a tree standing upside down (i.e) the root is in the air. (That is some imagination !) Let us pursue it further. The Unix File System has also its starting point as 'root' which is denoted by '/'. From this point onwards the branching begins. (There is no trunk). The typical File System would look like this.

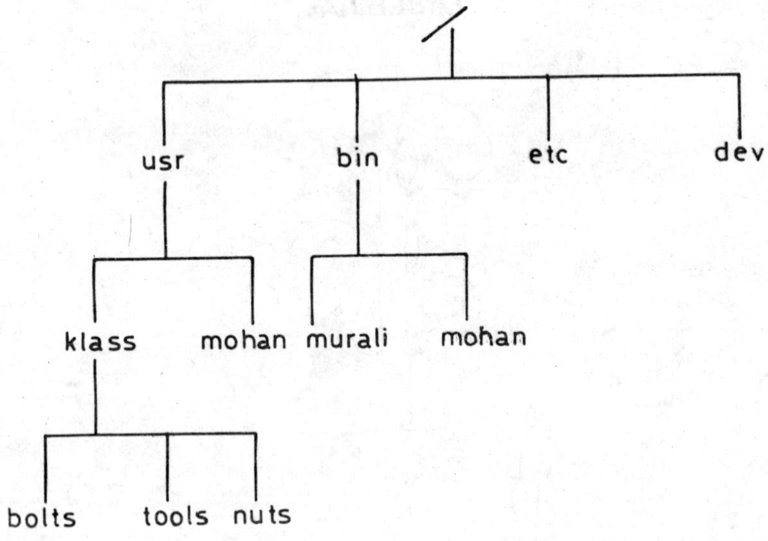

In the above '/' 'root' is considered as the principal or main directory. Then **usr, bin, etc, dev** represented as **/usr, /bin, /etc, /dev** respectively are directories under root. These in turn have files & subdirectories and so forth.

'tools' is a file under directory klass, which is itself a directory under '/usr'. **'usr'** in turn is a directory under root '/'. This kind of structure is called a hierarchial structure or a tree structure. The full name of the file tools is **/usr/klass/tools**. This is called the PATH NAME or the absolute PATH NAME of the file tools.

No two files in a directory can have the same name but files from different directories can have identical names, because the absolute path name is different for the two. For eg. as in the figure 2A "Mohan" is the file name for the two files in different directories. Their absolute path names are

- /usr/Mohan
/bin/mohan

As indicated above files can be addressed in two ways.

(i) THE ABSOLUTE PATH NAME which is the full name and begin with the root directory and works its way down to the file name.

(ii) THE RELATIVE PATH NAME: Here the file is addressed relating to the current working directory i.e. the directory where the present process is running. All references that do not begin with the "/" directory name are path names relative to the current working directory. Relative path names typically make use of two alternate names for directories. The first is (..) (dot dot) which refers to the parent directory and the second alternative is . (dot) which is another name for the present directory.

The Unix System has a regular set of directories which are as follows.

DIRECTORIES	CONTENTS
bin	Executable version of program is distributed with UNIX
dev	All special files or device files
etc	All files that are used by the system administrator.
lib	Contains the lib.a archive that holds the system calls & subroutines
tmp	The tmp directory is used to store all temporary files.
usr	All files pertaining to each user.

TABLE IIB

As mentioned earlier, the Unix System has four types of files. Let us adjourn to our tree, as we discuss the file types.

directory files These are files which tie together a group of files. The directory file can be written by the kernel only. When we create a new directory e.g., 'ndir', kernel makes an entry in this file **'ndir'** whenever a file is added to or deleted from the directory **'ndir'**. A directory file can be thought of as the branch e.g., **klass,** etc.

ordinary files These are files that contain data/information stored in any format and there is no specific order imposed on them. These files can be thought of as leaves in our UNIX tree.

fifo files Fifo files are those that let unrelated files communicate with each other. These files are typically used in applications where the communication path is only in one way and where a number of processes have to communicate with a single process, often called DAEMON PROCESS. Each process writes a message to the **fifo** file and the UNIX system guarantees that each individual message written on the file will not be overwritten by another user.

special files These are files that represent physical devices. They too can be thought of as leaves in the tree. When a process writes to a special file, the data is sent to the physical device associated with it. Special files are not really files but pointers that point to device drivers located in the kernel that handle data flow. A point to be noted is that since the physical devices are addressed as files the protection that is applicable to files is also applicable to physical devices. Before we conclude this chapter we will get acquainted with one file (ie) the Password file. We shall refer to this file in later chapters.

the password (/etc/passwd) file

Whenever a new user is created by the system administrator, or the super user, the following details have to be entered in the /etc/passwd file.

The password file has one password each for every user. Each record has several fields separated by (:). Following are the fields:

USER NAME (The name to be used at the time of login)
USER'S PASSWD - In an encrypted form (if any)
USER-ID (Each user is given a unique number by the system)
GROUP-ID (The number of the group to which the user belongs)
USER DESCRIPTION (Usually the user's full name)
HOME DIRECTORY (The user will be placed in this directory after logging into the system)
The process to be executed on logging in the system as user-By default the **/bin/sh** is executed.

conclusion

We have seen that the UNIX Operating System is not a single large program, but a combination of a small kernel which does low-level jobs, a shell and the file system. The kernel does not execute all the jobs itself but uses the other software tools or utilities that do all the peripheral work.

We have seen how the shell plays the role of an interpreter and finally we have had a look at how the files are classified and organised.

The last two chapters have been narrative in nature. You have been merely introduced to the UNIX Operating System and have had no active part to play. The subsequent chapters are more instructive and need complete involvement on your part. You should not remain just a "reader" but now you must become a "doer". You will get the best out of this book by following all the instructions and practically trying out the given problems. You can't learn swimming by just reading about it in a book. You have to jump into the water. Well now get set to tour the world of UNIX. All the BEST!

3

GETTING STARTED WITH UNIX - I

PRELUDE

We have seen the general functions of an operating system in chapter - I and in chapter- II 'Structure of Unix' we saw how the UNIX O.S. is organised. We also saw that we must communicate with the 'shell' in order to have our requests processed. Since the 'shell' plays the role of an interpreter it is natural to expect that the 'shell' will be able to understand any thing that you type as a command. This assumption is incorrect. The 'shell' expects you to follow a very strict discipline in terms of syntax. If the commands that you type in, are incorrect the system will either perform the wrong activity or politely inform you that you have entered an unknown command (It is quite polite fortunately, like a well groomed butler!). However the **'shell'** does permit you to write your own command syntax. As a well meaning programmer you can later write shell scripts which will let your fellow users use some easily understood syntax rather than the terse syntax understood by UNIX. But before we go on to 'doctoring' the 'shell' let us first understand the commands that are used to perform the various tasks in a data-processing environment.

OBJECTIVE:

In this chapter you will be introduced to the basic commands used in UNIX. Upon completing this chapter, you will be able to create a file, view it, count the number of words, delete a file, or rename it and so forth. You will also be able to create directories, navigate through directories etc.

Now get set to enter the UNIX world!
First let us login:

log-in

3.1 Logging in

Before you begin your "hands on" session on the UNIX system you have to first **"log in"**. The system administrator may have already done the necessary homework that will let you log in (You will learn all about this homework as you work through this material). When you sit before your terminal you will see the following:

```
login:
```

You now have to enter your login name or user ID. Login name or user ID is the name by which the UNIX system will identify you. After you have entered your login name (say mohan) you will see

```
login:mohan                    <Ret>
password:
```

The system is now prompting you to enter your password **(THE SYSTEM ADMINISTRATOR WILL TELL YOU YOUR LOGIN NAME & PASSWORD).** The password entered will not be displayed (it is supposed to be a secret!) on the screen. If you do not enter the password correctly the system will ask you to **"login"** once again. Once you enter the correct password, the system will display the following:

```
login:mohan                      <Ret>
password:                        <Ret>
Mon;Nov 19 10:10 1991
Welcome to Klass Computers
Please logout at the end of your session by pressing ^d.
$
```

You have logged in. Congratulations!

As you login, after you give your password, the system will automatically put you on to your **"HOME"** Directory. When you are given an account by the super user, he will allot a directory for you to work in. Each user will have a directory that is unique. This directory is called the HOME directory.

3.2.

HOME Your home directory is that directory under /**usr** which has been assigned to you. This is the directory that you will work in as soon as you login. Recall the /**etc**/**passwd** file that we discussed in "Structure of Unix". Your login directory or HOME directory will be recorded in this file. If you type

```
$ echo $HOME          <Ret>
  /usr/train
$
```

The name of your **'login'** directory is displayed. You can take this to be the starting point from where you will begin to move around the Unix system. However, as you continue to work, you will soon find yourself working in other directories too. In order to ascertain your exact location within the unix system use the **'pwd'** command.

3.3

pwd **print working directory**

To know which directory you are in type

```
$ pwd                 <Ret>
  /usr/train
$
```

PRESENT WORKING DIRECTORY

pwd

The command **'pwd'** displays the directory you are working in. **'pwd'** represents 'print working directory'. This means that you are now in directory **"train"** which is a subdirectory of "usr" which is a directory under **"root"**. Now that you have got your bearings. Let us see what files we have in your directory type the following:

```
$ ls          <Ret>
$
```

3.4 ls

list files in directory
[ls {-lairtduR}]

'ls' stands for list, and this command gets the system to display the list of files in the directory you are referring to. In this case since no directory is specified, the default directory is your current directory (i.e

/usr/train). The system has not displayed anything, but another **'$'** prompt has come on. This means that there are no files in your directory **/usr/train.** This is not surprising since your account is a new account. You have not done any work so far.

Let us create a file.

Now plelase remember that a file can be created using any of the editors avaialble under UNIX or simply by using **'cat'**. Chapter V deals exclusively with the editor **'vi'**. But at the moment we will work with **"cat"**.

Let us first create a file using '**cat**'. Because this is so much simpler.

CAUTION: (1) **THE COMMANDS GIVEN SHOULD BE TYPED EXACTLY AS THEY ARE.**

(2) UNIX IS *CASE SENSITIVE* (i.e.) A & a ARE TREATED AS DIFFERENT CHARACTERS.

```
$ cat > games        <Ret>
  Football
  Hockey
  Cricket
  Tennis
  Squash
  Polo
  Ctrl D
$
```

NOTE: *Ctrl and "D" pressed simultaneously will save the file and bring you back to system prompt*

- After you type [cat > games <Ret>] the cursor will jump to the next line and wait for your command. Enter the above as it is. We will be using this small file in many of the illustrations that follow.

To see if the file is really there in our directory type

```
$ ls                <Ret>
games
$
```

There you are! We have a file by name '**games**' in our directory!! You may often have to take a listing of files in your directory. Unix has a wide range of options to the **"ls"** command. Some of the often used options are listed in TABLE III A.

You may not need to know all of them right away. But go through the table to get an idea of the various options under ls.

LISTING OPTIONS

OPTION	ACTION
ls -a	lists all directories including "." entries
ls -i	lists files with i node numbers
ls -l	lists in long form
ls -r	lists files in reverse order
ls -t	lists files sorted by last modified time
ls -u	lists file sorted by last access time
ls -lt	list file in long form sorted by last modified time
ls -R	recursive list of all files in all subdirectories

TABLE IIIA

wild card characters

3.4.1

"?"

If a particular range of files have to be listed you can make use of wild card characters like **"?"** & **"*".** If you want to see all files with names having single characters, you would type

```
$ ls ? <Ret>
$
```

All files with names like "a", "b", "c" etc., would get listed. (Since you do not have any such file, nothing has been listed.). Assume that we have some other files. Next if you type

```
$ ls ??          <Ret>
  bk
  kb
$
```

This means file names with two characters have to be displayed. So a "?" will match any single character in a name.

3.4 2

"*"

Let us assume that you also have files with names like **games1, games2, gamesx, games500, gamesxyz, agames, abcgames, kidgames, biggames** and **mgames.** Type

```
$ ls games*                <Ret>
  games1
  games2
  gamesx
  games500
  gamesxyz
$
```

3.5

cp **copy file(s)**

[cp {Source file} {target file}]

Next let us copy the file **games** to another file **games1.** Type

```
$ cp games games1          <Ret>
$
```

Now Type

```
$ ls                       <Ret>
  games
  games1
$
```

Now we have two files, namely **games** & **games1.** The UNIX system belives in the principle 'NO NEWS IS GOOD NEWS !!'. You may have observed that after the file **'games'** was copied to file **'games1'** the system did not inform us in any way that it has successfully finished copying the file. Instead the prompt came on so that we could enter our next command. However if you were to type the following

```
$ cp hema games1           <Ret>
  cp:hema not found.
$
```

Hence UNIX feels it necessary to inform you only about that command which is not executed, either because the file named is incorrect or there is an error of syntax.

Let us do some more work on the "**cp**" command. During the course of your day to day work you will ofte ave to copy the contents of one file into another within your own directory or across directories. If you are copying files within your own directory then the syntax is the same as the syntax used when we copied file "**games**" to file '**games1**'.

```
$ cp {source file(s) } {target file}
```

While copying files across directories you will have to supply the full pathname of the target file or source file or both. Assume that you want to copy the file '**games**' from your directory **/usr/train/mohan** to a file '**names**' in the directory **/usr/bus/ram** then this is what you do:

```
$ cp /usr/train/moham/games   /usr/bus/ram/names <Ret>
$
```

That was a long command was it not? Suppose you wanted to copy a file '**sachin**' from the directory **/usr/train/giri** to your directory the type

```
$ cp /usr/train/giri/sachin          <Ret>
```

The unix system substitutes the '.' with the name of your present directory. (Recall that we mentioned in Chapter-II that the '.' represents your present directory). Actually when you copied the file '**games**' to the directory **/usr/bus/ram** you need not have typed the full path name of the source file. The following command would also do the job.

```
$ cp games  /usr/bus/ram/names          <Ret>
$
```

This will copy the file '**games**' from your directory to the file named '**names**' in the directory '**ram**'.

Now if you want that the target file in another directory to have the same name as the source file ie '**games**', then in that case simply type

```
$ cp games  /usr/bus/ram          <Ret>
$
```

NOTE: *The above commands will work only if you have the relevant permissions to access the files and directories that we mentioned here. Permissions and how to deal with them will be introduced to you in Chapter IV.*

Now let us look at the contents of **'games1'.** You can look at the contents of the **games1** by typing

```
$ cat games1              <Ret>
  Football
  Hockey
  Cricket
  Tennis
  Squash
  Polo
$
```

Since no purpose (at present) is served in having two files with identical contents, we might as well delete one file and clear up space for other files which we are going to create or copy from other directories.

3.6

wc **perform word count**
[wc {-lwc} {file name}]

But before we pack this file away, you could as well see the number of characters, words & lines that are there in games1. In order to do this, type

```
$ wc games1               <Ret>
  6 6 37 games1
$
```

The above means that the file **games1** contains six lines, six words and thirty seven characters. Whatever be the size of the file, **"wc"** will give you the answer in the same sequence (i.e) number of lines, number of words & number of characters and the file name which was processed.

Suppose you only wanted to know the number of words or the number of characters or only the number of lines in a file, then you can use the **"wc"** command with its options.

There are three options which have been described below:

```
$ wc -l games1          <Ret>
  6 games1
$
```

When you use the -l option you get the number of lines in the file **'games1'.**

```
$ wc -w games1                <Ret>
  6 games1
$
```

The **-w** option gives you the total number of words, which is also six. Ofcourse to get the number of characters, you must type

```
$ wc -c games1             <Ret>
  37 games1
$
```

3.7 rm

delete file(s)
[rm {file name(s)}]

It was decided earlier that we do not have to retain **'games1'.** To delete **'games1'** type

```
$ rm games1       <Ret>
$
```

Again you will notice that UNIX has not told you as to what it has done with regard to your command **"rm games1"**. It has simply displayed the next prompt. UNIX is definitely not communicative!

Now type

```
$ ls            <Ret>
  games
$
```

There you are ! There is only one file (i.e.) **'games'.** No sign of **'games1'.** Well, you just deleted it, did you not ! You have so far created a file, made a copy of the file, counted the number of lines, characters & words and then finally deleted the copy you made. If there is any doubt as to how you do the above, it is not a bad idea to once again go over the ground covered so far.

We have used the command **'cat'** with two variations so far. The first with the > symbol and the second without the > symbol. Log off now by pressing ^D while going through the following. [Nothing profound but something important]

Every command has a source of input and a target for output. The usual source of input is the keyboard because this is where you type in the commands. The output of the executed command is the terminal or rather the V.D.U. For example when you typed **[cat>games]** the system waits for you to enter something on the key board. You then entered football, hockey ... Later you typed **'cat games'** (without >) and viewed the contents of your file. In the first case the redirection operation > declared **'games'** as the standard output. So whatever you typed before ctrl 'D' was directed to the file **'games'.** (If **'games'** does not exist it is created, if it exists, then the file is overwritten). In the second case since no redirection operator is present the file games was treated as input and the output was the screen. So we could see the contents of the file **'games'.**

If you have logged off, login again and try the following

```
$ cat                    <Ret>
  Football
  Football
  Hockey
  Hockey
  Cricket
  Cricket
  Ctrl D
$
```

Rather irritating, is it not, like a parrot that repeats whatever you say. Actually what happened was, that since no output file was specified the **'cat'** command took the input from the keyboard (Standard.input) and displayed the output on to the screen (Standard output). That is why you see the system repeating whatever you type on the keyboard. We will talk more about redirection in later chapters.

Let us look at file handling again. Type

```
$ ls                <Ret>
  games
$
```

Remember we have only one file. The second file that we had was removed by typing

```
$ rm games1         <Ret>
$
```

3.7

mv

rename file(s)

[mv {oldfile} {newfile}]

When re-organising your files or just about anytime you will need to rename some of your files. Let us create another file and take a look at how files are renamed. Here we go!

To create another file, type

```
$ cat > birds       <Ret>
  sparrow
  eagle
  parrot
  peacock
  kiwi ("Ctrl d")
$
```

To rename the file **'birds'** to **'feathers'** type

```
$ mv bird feathers          <Ret>
$
```

What happens actually is the file **'birds'** is copied to the file **'feathers'** and the original file **'birds'** is removed.

Create a third file by typing

```
$ cat > birds1          <Ret>
  emu ("Ctrl d")
$
```

Let us list the files in our directory. Type

```
$ ls              <Ret>
  games
  feathers
  birds1
$
```

Let us rename the file **'feathers'** to **'birds'.** Type

```
$ mv feathers birds       <Ret>
$
```

Now type

```
$ ls              <Ret>
  games
  birds
  birds1
$
```

3.8

redirection with cat

To append one file to another or to copy the contents of file1 to file2 at the end of file2, type

```
$ cat birds > >  birds1      <Ret>
$
```

Recall that the file **"birds1"** had only one record (i.e) **"emu"**. Now let us see the contents of **"birds1"**. Type

```
$ cat birds1            <Ret>
  emu
  sparrow
  eagle
  parrot
  peacock
  kiwi
$
```

Observe that the contents of file **'birds'** have got appended to the file **"birds1".** This was the case of appending one file to another. How do we append two files onto a third file? First let us create another file.

Type ·

```
$ cat > kids          <Ret>
  kitten
  puppy
  cubs ("Ctrl D")
$
```

To appendfile **'kids'** & file **'birds'** to file **'kb'** type

```
$ cat kids birds > > kb        <Ret>
$
```

Now, to look at the contents of **'kb'**, type

```
$ cat kb              <Ret>
  kitten
  puppy
  cubs
  sparrow
  eagle
  parrot
  peacock
  kiwi
$
```

Next type

```
$ cat birds kids > > bk          <Ret>
$
```

Let us see the contents of file **bk,** type

```
$ cat bk             <Ret>
  sparrow
  eagle
  parrot
  peacock
  kiwi
  kitten
  puppy
  cubs
$
```

The difference between two two files, **'kb'** & **'bk'** should be clear to you. The purpose of this illustration was to bring home the fact that the order of arguments for a particular command are very important. If this is not observed you are likely to get unexpected results.

3.9

mkdir :

create new directory

[mkdir {directory name}]

As you do more and more work, you will add more and more files. It is a good practice to classify the files and keep them under different directories. E.g. one directory containing program files, another containing letters and so forth. To make new directory, type

```
$ mkdir prog          <Ret>
$
```

Next we must change from current directory to the new directory. Type

```
$ cd prog          <Ret>
$
```

To see our current directory, type

```
$ pwd        <Ret>
  /usr/train/prog
$
```

3.10

cd

change directory

[cd {directory name}]

While we are on the subject of directories remember that [(. .) (dot dot)] means parent directory & [(.) (dot)] means your present directory. The parent directory of **/prog** is **/usr/train.** This is also your HOME directory. To go back to the parent directory, type

```
$ cd..        <Ret>
$
```

Alternately you can use '**cd**' without any argument to go back to your HOME directory regardless of your present location in the Unix system.

3.11

rmdir :

remove directory
[rmdir {directory name}]

When you do housekeeping on your system, you will be getting rid of old files and directories. When you have removed all the files in a directory, you come to its parent directory and remove the empty directory. This is how

```
$ rmdir prog          <Ret>
$
```

Now type

```
$ cd prog             <Ret>
  directory not found
$
```

Now let us do some work on the data/text within a given file(s). For this purpose, we may have to create a few more files. First let us take a listing of the files in our directory. Type

```
$ ls              <Ret>
  games
  birds
  kids1
  bk
  kb
  prop
$
```

3.12

pg

display file pagewise
[pg {file name}]

If you have a file that is a large text file, and if you wanted to go through it without using an editor it would be very difficult. If the **"cat"** command is used the contents will simply scroll up. You can use **"Ctrl S"** to arrest the scrolling and **"Ctrl Q"** to resume scrolling. But this method is not elegant. Instead you can use the **"pg"** command. If the large file in question is named **"prop",** then type:

```
$ pg prop      <Ret>
```

This command **"pg"** will display the file page by page. (One page is 24 lines on most VDU's). After displaying one screenful of text, the system will pause and let you read the text. Once you are through, press enter key and the next screenful will be displayed. If you press **"q"** the system will come out of the **"pg"** program and display system prompt.

3.13

pipe

While still pursuing the above subject, we will briefly touch an important facility called **"pipe"**. This is not something that you smoke, but a means of conveying the output of one command as an input to the next command and so forth. Supposing you have a very large directory and entered **"ls"**, the directory of files will simply scroll away. Using **"Ctrl S"** & **"Ctrl Q"** will help but it is not the ideal method. So we must try to 'paginate' this file. There are two ways to do this (1) Type

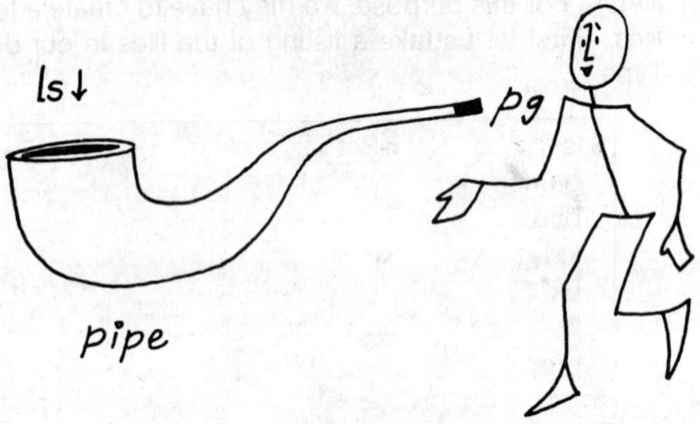

pipe

```
$ ls * > test          <Ret>
$
```

We are redirecting the output of **"ls"** to a file **'test'.** Now type

```
$ pg test          <Ret>
```

The display is paginated.

The second method illustrates the use of "pipes" which pipes the output of one command as the input of the next. Also a lot of temporary file creation is avoided.

(2) Type

```
$    ls    |     pg                    <Ret>
     |     |     |
     |     |     Paginate command
     |     piping
    list directory
```

The "|" pipes or conveys the output of the command **"ls"** to the command **"pg"** which paginates the output. Any number of **"pipes"** can be used in a command sequence. But use it cautiously or you may not get the right results.

We will do more work on pipes later

Miscellaneous commands

Some of the commands that follow do not really fit into the scheme of things discussed so far. They will come in use when we program the **"shell".** However go through these commands now, you can refer to them later.

3.14

echo

display argument
[echo {argument}]

"echo" displays the arguments on the screen. For example if you type

```
$ echo "How are you"  <Ret>
  How are you
$
```

"echo" also displays the contents of a variable if the variable name is preceeded with a **"$".** We were able to get the name of our HOME directory (3.2) by using the "echo" command.

```
$ echo $HOME            <Ret>
  /usr/train
$
```

This command will come in use when we write shell scripts. It is a good practice to enclose the message in double quotes.

SIGNIFICANCE OF QUOTES / CHARACTER IN ECHO

CHARACTER	IMPLICATIONS
"	Removes special meaning of ',,,#,*,?,&,|,;,(,),[,],^. Blank line,\,space, tabs are interpreted.
'	Remove the meaning of above and,$,\,'.
\	Remove special meaning of character that follows.
`	Causes enclosed command to be executed.

Further option of echo are as follows. The character \n,\c,\t as part of the message can change the display.

OPTIONS	
\n	This will create a new line after the text is displayed
\c	The cursor will stay on the same line
\t	The cursor will move to next tab position

3.15

sleep You would like a particular message or output on the screen to be displayed for a while, before proceeding with the next display. This is achieved by delaying the next step in the program by the required interval. Within a shell script a command like **"sleep 5**" will execute the subsequent step after five seconds.

3.16

nice

change process priority
[nice -n program name]

You will appreciate the advantages of **"sleep"** when you design an application program. **"sleep"** as we have seen suspends execution of a program from within. But suppose you have to submit a program for execution, but you want it to run after the other programs, that are presently running or are going to be executed, you can use the **"nice"** command. The **"nice"** command allocates a lower priority to the job which we want to run. The highest priority is O & the lowest is 120. Usually jobs run at a priority level of 20. Only a super user can run a job at a priority higher than 20 (e.g) 15. In order to run the program **'DDrecon'** at a priority of '25', type

```
$ nice -5 DDrecon &      <Ret>
  510
$
```

The '-5' in the command means, reduce the priority by '5', so the program **'DDrecon'** will run with a priority of '25'. The '&' is used to get the P.I.D. (Process I.D. remember we discussed in Chapter-II that P.I.D is a unique number alloted to a process when it is initiated.)

3.17

kill

terminate process
[kill -n P.I.D.]

The P.I.D can be used by the **"kill"** command if necessary. As you will see when you write your shell scripts that some scripts will continue to execute in a never ending loop. A (Ctrl D) will also not be able to abort the program. Also we can't ask everybody to log off and reset the system. To our rescue comes the **"kill"** command. Following is the syntax

```
$ kill -n m        <Ret>
```

where '**n**' is the **"kill"** signal and 'm' is the P.I.D.

Usually the **"kill"** signal **'9'** is given which is the most effective. **'15'** is the default signal but sometimes the process can **'trap'** this signal. If you want to kill the **'DDrecon'** program,

type

```
$ kill -9 510        <Ret>
  510 killed/terminated
$
```

3.18

ps **process status**

[ps { -altname}]

But then everybody may not have used **"nice"** and **'&'** with their command which prompts the system to respond with the P.I.D. number. So if you want to know all the process running on the system, type

```
$ ps -al        <Ret>
```

```
FSUIDPIDPPIDCPRINIADDRSZWCHANTTYTIMECOMD
04R10016510500675254ce0064tty011.15DDrecon
10R10117415396060204d006tty090.30qrou
```

You are perhaps wondering what this is all about. What you are seeing is the detailed info of the processes running on your system. Most of the information presented here is an overkill as far as the normal user is concerned. Perhaps the system administrator may need some of the information. Let us take each heading and confirm to ourselves that what we are seeing is not anything abnormal.

F Process Flags
01 In core
02 System's swapper process
04 Process locked in RAM
10 Process being swaped
20 Process being traced

S Process status
S sleeping
O Non existent
W Waiting
R Running
I Intermediate
Z Terminated

UID	Process owners user I.D.
PID	Process I.D.
PPID	ID of parent process
C	Processor utilisation for scheduling
PRI	Priority of the process
NI	Used in priority computation
ADDR	Memory address of process. Disc address if process not in memory.
SZ	Process memory images size in 512 byte blocks
WCHAN	The event for which the process is sleeping or waiting
TTY	The terminal controlling the process
TIME	Cumulative execution time
COMD	The command and its arguments

It is not very complicated really, but there is more info than we need as users. So let us look at the other options of ps.

OPTIONS	**ACTIONS**
-a	Report info about all process (short form)
-l	Report info in the long format
-tname	Report process controlled by terminal name

If no option is specified, processes initiated by the user are displayed.

```
$ ps               <Ret>
  PID   TTY   TIME  COMD
  17    tty19 21    sh       → user's shell
  57    tty19 01    ps       → This ps command
$
```

That is the **"ps"** command and how it is to be used with the **"kill"** & **"nice"** command. Well, enough of **"nice"** & **"kill"**, let us look at the **"date"** command.

3.19

date **display/set system date & time**
[date]

This command is used to set the date & time or to get a display of system date & time. Type

```
$ date               <Ret>
  Thu Jan 15 12:56:25 1983
$
```

To set a new date, type

```
$ date [MMddhhmmyy]     <Ret>
$
```

MM - Month: dd - date: hh - hour: mm - minute: yy - year

```
$ date '-TIME : % H : % M : % S'        <Ret>
  TIME : 15:50:35
$
```

Alternate options for date		
m	-	month of year in digits
d	-	day of month
y	-	last digits of year
H	-	hrs in the airline format
M	-	minutes upto 59
S	-	seconds upto 59
T	-	full time in the format hh:mm:ss
j	-	day of the year 0 to 365
a	-	abbreviated form of the day
R	-	time in am/pm

3.20

cal **display calendar**
[cal n]

Used to get a calendar for the month. Type

```
$ cal 3  <Ret>  (To get the calendar displayed
                 for the month of March 1991).
$
```

If **"cal"** is typed without any arguments, the calendar for the current year is displayed. Type

```
$ cal 1989 <Ret> (will display the calendar for 1989)
$
```

3.21

banner

display argument in banner form
[banner {argument}]

The command **"banner"** displays its argument in the form of a banner (i.e.) it creates a large matrix of "#" in the shape of the characters of the argument.

```
$ banner E          <Ret>
  ##########
  #
  #
  ######
  #
  #
  ##########
$
```

The output of the banner can be redirected to a file and viewed when required.

Well that concludes the first 'hands on' session with Unix. Go through the various commands once again if you like. By doing so you will make sure that you have not misunderstood any of the command syntax. Before going on to the next chapter let us look at the commands covered so far.

pwd	print working directory
ls	list files in directory
HOME	Your login directory
cat	create/view/concatenate files
rm	delete file
mkdir	create directory
rmdir	remove directory
mv	rename file

wc	perform 'word count' on a file
ps	list current processes
pg	paginate file
|	piping output
echo	display argument
sleep	suspend execution of process
nice	change process priority
kill	terminate process
date	to display/set system time
cal	display calendar
banner	display argument in banner form

That is not bad at all. We have covered quite a bit. Now complete the exercise and proceed to the next chapter.

GETTING STARTED WITH UNIX - I

EXERCISE

1. How many characters can you display in banner format side by side?
2. What is the use of having a command called "sleep"?
3. How will you terminate a job if it is running in the background?
4. What is the difference between "cp" command and the "mv' command?
5. What are the options for the "wc" command?
6. When should you use the quotations (single or double) within an echo statement?
7. In your HOME directory create two new directories called ndir and odir.
8. Use cat to create a file called "xyz".
9. Copy the file xyz to the directory ndir.
10. Delete the file xyz from your directory.
11. Copy the file xyz from the ndir directory to the directory odir without changing the present working directory.
12. Try out the "ls" commands with all its options.
13. Remove the directory odir.
14. Create another file abc using cat.
15. Append the file abc to xyz.
16. Create a file "mno" such that its contents are the contents of abc followed by the contents of xyz.
17. List all the process running on the system.
18. What is your PID?
19. When should you use the "&" when issuing a command?

20. How will you display all the files in the system?

21. How will you delete all the files in your directory using a single command? The system should prompt you for an yes or no to delete each file.

22. When are FIFO file created?

23. Go to the / directory. How will you display the directory page by page?

24. Write down two advantages of using the pipe " | " command?

25. List all files which have filename with only two characters.

26. List out all .c files.

27. List out all files whose names start with "m".

4

GETTING STARTED WITH UNIX - II

Welcome to the second phase of Getting Started with UNIX. In the last Chapter we dealt with UNIX commands that were very simple. You were told how to create a file, a directory, how to change directories, copy files across directories and so forth. In this chapter you can look forward to some more interesting commands.

OBJECTIVE: This chapter will introduce you to commands for file comparison, string search, file location and extraction of selected records and fields from a file. Next, the basics of file security are discussed. Also upon completion of this chapter you will understand the concept of permissions on files. Further, you will be able to set permission for your files as you see fit.

You are perhaps feeling like Robinson Crusoe, working all alone in the world of UNIX. There is no one to talk to or to share your thoughts with. Don't loose heart. You will find more than your share of Man Fridays.

4.1 who

list logged in users

[who {am i}]

The UNIX Operating System is a multiuser, multitasking operating system. This means that more than one user can work on the system. There is a possibility that somebody else, sitting in another room is logged on to your system. In order to see who else is working on your system, type

```
$ who                          <Ret>
  01 10:05
  kumar  tty014  Nov 01 10:17
  ram    tty019  Nov 01 10:31
  vicky  tty012  Nov 01 11:01
$
```

You see above, that four persons including yourself have logged onto the system. The terminal number is followed by the date which is the current system date and the login time. In the above example the date is the same. (i.e.) Nov 01. However, if for example Mr. Ram had logged on to the system on Oct 31 at 23:10 then the last login date and time would be displayed. To see your own terminal number and login time type

4.1.1

who am i

```
$ who am i                    <Ret>
  mohan  tty011  Nov 01 10:05
$
```

Now you know who you are and also the other users who are presently logged on to the system. If you want to send a message to Kumar who is sitting two floors above you, you can simply "WRITE" a message to him. Here's how. Type

```
$ write kumar          <Ret>
```

4.2

write **send message to user**

[write {user name}]

Upon giving this command Mr.Kumar is alerted. On his screen he will get a display as follows [Whatever Kumar is doing at the moment will be interrupted.]

```
message from mohan tty011
```

You can now type the message that you want to send. It can be as long as you like and must be terminated by a **"Ctrl d"**

```
$ write kumar <Ret>
  Hi kumar, This is to remind
  you that we have to visit
  Venkat today ("Ctrol d")
```

Kumar's terminal will display the following

```
Message from mohan tty 011
Hi Kumar, this is to remind you that we have to visit
Venkat today.
```

We have just seen the **"write"** command. You will observe that to initiate a dialogue with another user is very easy. But this ease of starting a pow-vow with another user can cause a lot of disturbance and irritation.

If, for example you are working on an important document or a complicated program, a message saying "what has banks but no money?" can be very irritating. To avoid such interruptions type

```
$ mesg n <Ret>
$
```

4.3

mesg **change access status**

[mesg { y/n }]

This means (MESSAGE NO)

If someone were to send you a message thus:

```
$ write mohan          <Ret>
  What did one wall say to another ? ("Ctrl d")
```

This user would get a message

```
"Access denied" or "Permission denied"
$
```

Later if you want to make yourself accessible to other users you should type

```
$ mesg y  <Ret>
$
```

Now the others can start a parley with you.

4.4 mail

mail

send mail to user
[mail {user name}]

Most users do not type in **"mesg y"** which means that we cannot access them using **'write'**. Moreover, in order to use **"write"** the receiver must be logged on. So, how do you send a message without using **"write"** or leave a message for someone who has not yet logged on to the system? UNIX provides us with a facility called **"mail".** As you login you will see a message before the prompt is displayed :

```
you have mail
$
```

If, at the prompt you enter

```
$ mail  <Ret>
```

The system will now look into your 'mailbox' to see the mail sent to you by the other users. Messages are displayed one by one in reverse chronological order.

```
$ mail
  1. message
  1. kumar Mon Dec 2 10:13 8/116 "letr"
```

{At this stage the system will wait for your response. Press p.}

```
  p
  From Kumar. Mon Dec 02 10:13 1991
  To Mohan
  Sub: letr
  Dated: Mon Dec 02 10:13 1991
  Message: Will you please confirm the demo date for
  FAC Sys. {Again the system will pause for your
  response Refer to table for response}.
```

After each message is displayed, the system will wait for a command from the user so that the message can be disposed off accordingly. The prompt is in the form of a question mark **'?'**. (In some implementations the cursor merely pauses). You can either delete the message or save it in a file or quit from the program. The display of messages is in the LIFO form (Last in First Out). TABLE IVA gives a limited set of commands.

OPTION	MEANING
<Ret>	No disposition on this message. It will be available when the mail is read the next time. Next message is displayed.
d	Delete this message. Next message is displayed.
s{filename}	Save message in filename. Display next message.
q	quit mail; Unread messages remain in mailbox Back to system prompt $

TABLE IV - A

You can send mail to your fellow user just as you sent a message using **"write".** This is how

```
$ mail kumar                  <Ret>
  subject: DEMO by T & Co
  We have to go and see a demo of the new Package
  on Financial Accounting developed by Timbuctoo &
  Co. Please make sure you do not have any other
  engagements on 12-12-91.
  Ctrl d
$
```

Now Kumar can view the message by using the **"mail"** command without any arguments. You can store the message in a file and send the same to more than one user in one stroke. This is how

```
$ mail kumar ram vicky  < <visit  <Ret>
$
```

Here **"visit"** is the name of the file which contains the message. It is redirected using the redirection operator.

DIFFERENCE BETWEEN MAIL & WRITE

At the beginning of the session you were informed about mail thus:

```
you have mail
$
```

And by simply typing **"mail"** you were able to read the messages in the mailbox. **"write"** is a dynamic program (i.e) it can be initiated anytime you like and terminated anytime you like. But mail looks into your mailbox periodically and informs you about it. The mailcheck is done at intervals and the length of the interval can be set.

Secondly you can send mail even if the user is not logged on to the system. But this cannot be done with **"write"**. **"mail"** informs you about the presence of MAIL on two occassions. First when you log in. Second when you receive a message from a fellow-user. However it will not interrupt your work, but will wait untill you are finished with the command that you are presently working on.

Finally you can save the message that is sent through the **"mail"** but you cannot do so with **"write"**.

We have so far seen how to find out the users who have logged in, how to communicate with them and how to avoid being disturbed by a talkative colleague.

Now on to files.

Files maintained by us have data on the various aspects of our business. There will be customer's details, supplier's details, employee details and more. We should be able to view these files and extract relevent records as dictated by events. Usually we rely on readymade packages or customised programs for this. However UNIX has an assortment of utilities which help us on this front. Some of them we will discuss in this chapter and others in later chapters. But before we begin work on files let us first 'find' the files to work on. As they say "First catch your hare". Let us see how to 'find' a file.

4.5

find **locate file(s)**

[find {directory} option {file name} -print]

We sometimes have to refer a file, but we do not know in which directory/subdirectory it is. It is not practical to go through every directory in order to locate the file. Unix provides a facility in the form of **"find"**. The **"find"** command comes with a number of options. The search can be made on a name, access time, modified time etc.,

"find" also permits the use of wild card characters. To find a file with name **bk,** searching from the root, type

```
$ find / -name bk -print  <Ret>
  /usr/train/bk
$
```

The full path name of the directory is printed, if the file is found. Let us find all files that have been modified 5 days ago (The search must start from **/usr)** The **"find"** command is not very talkative. It will quietly do its bit and not tell you weather it is successful or otherwise. You have to specifically use the **[-print]** option to get a display of the full pathname of the file located. Otherwise you would not know if the search has borne fruit or not.

```
$ find /usr -type f -mtime 5 -print  <Ret>
                                  └→ display the names
                               5 days ago
                       modified time
              file type-ordinary
      search from /usr directory
```

The options for **"find"** are as follows

OPTION	FUNCTION
-atime n	The file accessed "n" days before
-mtime n	The file was modified "n" days ago
-exec 'command'\;	Execute 'command' for all files that meet the conditions of find
-name filename	Name of the file to find
-newer filename	The file being searched must be 'newer' thus the filename referred
-links n	The file must have 'n' links
-ok 'command'	Execute 'command' for each successful find. But confirm with user before execution.
-print	Display on screen complete path name of file that meets the 'find' condition.
-size 'n'	files whose block size is n.
-type 'c'	Type of file, if 'd' then directory, if 'f' then ordinary file. ['c' in character, 'n' is integer + n means more than 'n' -n means less than 'n' ! negates the condition

OK! We have found the file which has to be referred to. There are a number of ways to refer to it. Remember we used **"cat"**; then we used **"pg"** to view the file page by page. But UNIX has many more tricks in the bag. Let us now look at some of them.

4.6

headn

display first n lines of file
[head -n {file name}]

To look at the first two lines of a file, type

```
$ head -2 games  <Ret>
  Football
  Hockey
$
```

If the command **"head"** is used without any arguments, the first 10 lines of the file are displayed.

4.7

tail-n

display last n lines of file
[tail -n {file name}]

'tail' displays the last 10 lines of the file if no arguments are specified. To see the last three lines type

```
$ tail -3 games          <Ret>
  Tennis
  Squash
  Polo
$
```

4.8

more

display file
[more (options) {file name}]

Sometimes we may want to browse through a file, like the file **'prop'** that Hans wanted us to vet. We have seen **'tail'** & **'head'** commands, but these commands are not practical when we want to browse through a file. Unix has an utility called **'more'** which can be used as follows.

Type

```
$ more prop  <Ret>
  This proposal has you
very specific is
modular by con
very user friendly
8% 'prop' –
```

As seen in the hypothetical screen above, the **'more'** command displays a pageful of text. A page of text on a standard output is generally 24 lines by 80 columns. On the last line the percentage of the file and the name of the file is displayed. The **"more"** command comes with the following options

OPTIONS	FUNCTION
-n	display text upto 'n' line no.
-s	supress blank lines if more than one
+/ string	start paging from the first occurance of the string
h	display help screen.

Using **"head", "tail"** and **"more"** we have had a quick look at the contents of the file. But if you want to locate a file with a particular phrase or see if a particular phrase is present in a list of files then you need some more sophisticated commands. Let us now look at one of them.

4.9

grep **pattern matching**

[grep pattern {file name(s)}]

Now that you have found the file you would like to look for a particular word in the file. The syntax is

[grep pattern file(s)]

If you want to find the presence of a word say **'Jerry'** in the file **'cartoon'**, you would type

```
$ grep Jerry cartoon      <Ret>
  cartoon:
  Tom & Jerry is very entertaining
  Jerry is the name
  Butch befriends Jerry
  kicks Jerry one foot and two inches in
$
```

The grep command prints all the lines of the file which contain the string **'Jerry'.** **'grep'** can be used for pattern matching on more than one file by using wild card characters or by typing the file names one after another. Filename for each file, where the pattern is found will be displayed before the relevant lines are displayed. More about **'grep'** in the chapter on Special Utilities. What we have seen so far in the **"grep"** command was to locate a file with the particular string or to locate a string in a text file or data file. Next we will see how to manipulate a data file.

4.10
sort

sort file contents
[sort (options) {input file name} {output file name}]

To sort, means to arrange items (in our case, records) in a certain meaningful format. The format or order will depend upon certain attribute(s). For example you can sort your customer details in the order of highest sales. Here the sales figure is the key for sorting or arranging the customer records. UNIX also has a command to sort your files or data within a file(s). The **"sort"** command sorts the file based on one key field or on more than one key fields in the order specified. Since the sorting is done on a field it is necessary that each line of the file contains that field. Let us sort the file games. Type

```
$ sort games              <Ret>
  Cricket
  Football
  Hockey
  Polo
  Squash
  Tennis
$
```

Let us do a reverse sort.

Type

```
$ sort -r games          <Ret>
  Tennis
  Squash
  Polo
  Hockey
  Football
Cricket
$
```

"sort" has a number of options available. The table of options is given as under.

OPTIONS	FUNCTIONS
-f	Ignore case
-n	Sort the numeric strings arithmetically
-o filename	Output filename
-r	Do a reverse sort
-t"c"	'c' is the field seperator

In both the examples above, the file **"games"** was actually unaltered. The display that we saw as an output was however sorted in the order specified. If you want to save the sorted output into another file you must specifically do so by using the [-o filename] option.

Suppose you want to save the reverse sorted output of the file **"games"** into another file **"sports"** then this is what you do.

```
$ sort -r -o sports games      <Ret>
$
```

Now take a look at the file **"sports"**. Type

```
$ cat sports             <Ret>
  Tennis
  Squash
  Polo
  Hockey
  Football
  Cricket
$
```

When the number of fields are more than one, the key field(s) are denoted as "**+m -n**". This means the field to be sorted is "**+m**" fields from the first field and "**-n**" is the ending field number.

```
$ sort +1 -2 -o sortfile test1          <Ret>
        |  |  |          └→ File to be sorted.
        |  |  ↓
        |  ↓ Output file.
        ↓  Ending key field.
     Starting key field.
```

In the above example we see that by specifying [+1 -2] the first field should be skipped and the second field should be taken as the key field for sorting and the output must be directed to "**sortfile**". The input file is "**test1**". We will see some more illustration after seeing "**cut**".

4.11 **cut** **display selected fields**

[cut (-fc) {file name}]

The names of all the users of a system will appear in the **/etc/passwd** file. In order to sort the list cf users, we need only that field of each line which contains the user's full name. How do we get a display of the names only, or more generally how do we get the display of any particular field in a file. Let us first create a file.

```
$ cat > test1   <Ret>
  Mohan      34   klass Mylapore
  Azam       29   padmaja Mylapore
  Ramani     40   padmaja Saligramam
  Ananth     37   pams Adyar
  Kannan     37   sds T.Nagar
  Siraj      31   advent Triplicane
  Ctrl d
$
```

To display only the second field type

```
$ cut -d" " -f2 test1             <Ret>
  34
  29
  40
  37
  37
  31
$
```

To sort the above list in ascending order type

```
$ cat test1: cut -d" " -f2: sort -n         <Ret>
  29
  31
  34
  37
  37
  40
$
```

The output of **"cat"** was **"piped"** to **"cut"** which cut the second field and **"piped"** the output to **"sort"** which in turn sorted the input numerically. The piping has helped to reduce the number of intermediate steps and temporary files which have to be otherwise created. Note that we had to specify a delimiter in the case of **"cut".** In the case of sort we should specify a delimiter if it is something other than space. However if the space is more than one column then the treatment for that is something else. You will soon see what it is.

4.11.1

cut -c The **"-c"** option lets you cut the characters instead of fields. If you wanted to cut only the first four characters of each line of test1, type

```
$ cut -c1-4 test1           <Ret>
  Moha
  Azam
  Rama
  Anan
  Kann
  Sira
$
```

4.12

tr **trim/squeeze extra space**

[tr -s " " {file name}]

Every thing looks rosy and nice. Right! But there is a small hiccup. We have assumed that the file **"test1"** has only one space between its fields. What if there is more than one column of space between the fields. If this is the case, **"cut"** will not produce the correct results. There is a facility available to "squeeze" the extra space and then **"pipe"** the "squeezed" output to the next command.. Also if the delimiter is a **":"** instead of a space this can also be specified. Suppose you have a file **"test4"** which looks like this and you wanted to sort it as above then what do you do?

```
$ cat test4      <Ret>
  Mohan      34    klass       Mylap
  Azam       29    padmaja     Mylapore
  Ramani     40    padmaja     Saligramam
  Ananth     37    pams        Adyar
  Kannan     37    sds         T.Nagar
  Siraj      31    adwent      Triplicane
```

Type

```
$ cat test: tr -s " " :cut -d" " -f2 sort -n          <Ret>
        This does the squeezing
29
31
34
37
37
40
$
```

The **"tr"** command "squeezes" the space between the fields in the file and presents them to the **"cut"** command with only one space between the fields [Before performing cut or sort make sure of the delimiter]. If we have the field seperator as **":"** as in the case of **/etc/passwd** file you would type

```
$ cat /etc/passwd: cut -d":" -f3: sort -o new      <Ret>
$
```

Alternatively you can directly sort the **/etc/passwd** file which has **":"** as the field seperator as follows

```
$ sort -t":" +2 -3 -o new1 /etc/passwd             <Ret>
$
```

Take a look at the two files.

4.13

uniq **display unique lines**

[uniq (-udc) {file name}]

An everyday application is comparison of two or more files. You would like to see how they differ from one another and also if within files or a list of names if a name is repeated and if repeatead, how many times and so forth. To find out how many unique words or names are there in the file, you can use the **"uniq"** command. Before submitting the file to **"uniq"** sort the file. This will list the identical records one after another. Only then the **"uniq"** command will give the expected results. Following are the options

```
$ uniq [-udc] {filename}      <Ret>
         ||  ——→{ -c count of duplications }
         | { -d display of duplicate line }
        { -u only unique lines are displayed }
```

Let us try out an example using one of the files that has been created, type

```
$ ls                          <Ret>
  games
  birds
  kids
  birds1
  bk
  kb
  new
$
```

Let us first sort the file **"kb"**.

```
$ sort -o kb kb              <Ret>
$
```

The sorted output of the file is re-written to the file **"kb"** itself. Now to try out the **"uniq"** command, type

```
$ uniq -d kb                 <Ret>
$
```

What happened? Apparently nothing ! Observe that in the above command the option specified was **"-d"** (i.e) display of duplicate lines. This means that the file **"kb"** does not have any duplicate lines. By conclusion all lines are unique. Let us confirm. Type

```
$ uniq -u kb     <Ret>
  cubs
  eagle
  kitten
  kiwi
  parrot
  peacock
  puppy
```

Suppose we append the file **kids** with **kb** (By the way cat is an acronym for CONCATENATE). We will then see what happens when we use **"uniq"** . Type

```
$ cat kids > > kb                         <Ret>
$
```

Next sort the file **"kb"**.

```
$ sort kb -o kb                           <Ret>
$
```

Now let us try out **"uniq"**. Type

```
$ uniq -d kb                  <Ret>
  cubs
  kitten
  puppy
$
```

This means that the above lines are duplicated.

Now let us try out the "**-u**" option.

```
$ uniq -u kb                    <Ret>
  eagle
  kiwi
  parrot
  peacock
  sparrow
$
```

These are the unique lines. The "**-c**" option is an interesting one. It gives us a list of all the records in the file and also the number of times it has occured. Type

```
$ uniq -c kb   <Ret>
  2 cubs
  1 eagle
  2 kitten
  1 parrot
  1 peacock
  2 puppy
  1 sparrow
$
```

It tells us how many times a word is repeated. As an exercise '**cat**' the file "**kids**" to the above file once again and see for yourself the result of the "**-c**" option.

4.14

comm **file comparison**

[comm {file a} {file b}]

File comparison is an every day application. We would like to know which lines of file1 are present in file2. For example if you are preparing a list of customers, you would like to see the difference between the new and old list. Create two files "**a**" and "**b**" as follows.

```
$ cat > a                    <Ret>
  siraj
  kannan
  govi
  paddu
  ramani
   ^d
$
```

```
$ cat > b                    <Ret>
  siraj
  kannan
  govi
  paddu
  mohan
   ^d
$
```

Now type

```
$ comm a b              <Ret>
  ramani
           mohan
                         siraj
                         kannan
                         govi
                         paddu
$
```

The output is in three columns. The first column contains lines unique to file **"a"**. The second column contains lines unique to file **"b"**. The third column contains lines common to both.

4.14.1

options

```
comm [-1 2 3] file1 file2
            |  |  |
            |  |  don't include column 3 in output
            |  don't include column 2 in output
         don't include column in output.
```

4.15

cmp **file comparison**

[cmp {file a} {file b}]

We have seen that the **"uniq"** command checks for unique lines in a file and **"comm"** compares two files where you have the option to print out the lines that are common to both files. The **"cmp"** command compares the files and reports at which point the files differ. The output is in the form of byte & line number.

```
$ cat  >c                    <Ret>
  This is a test
  Ctrl d
$
```

```
$ cat > d                    <Ret>
  This was a test  ("Ctrl d")
$
```

Now to compare the two files.

```
$ cmp c d  <Ret>
  c d differ : character 6 line 1
$
```

Go through the above once again if necessary and then we will move on to File Security.

4.16 **FILE SECURITY**

Your friend once asks you to examine a proposal he is preparing and says that the name of the file is **"prop"** and the directory is **"cust".** The directory **"cust"** is a subdirectory of **/usr.** Your home directory is also a subdirectory of /**usr.** To see the contents of his file **"prop"**, you will type

```
$ cat prop                    <Ret>
  prop:permission denied
$
```

What? You have been denied permission! Let us take a closer look at the attribute of the file **"prop"** Type

```
$ ls -l prop                  <Ret>
  -rwx– – –  1 hans class 540 Nov 10 15:10 prop
$
```

Before we examine the output of this command, let us examine the command itself.

```
$ ls -l prop  <Ret>
  |  |   └──→ prop : file name
  |  ↓
  |  -l : long form
  ↓
  ls : directory listing
```

When we specify this option (-l) we get the following details of the file.

```
$ ls -l prop                  <Ret>
  -rwx– – –  1 hans  class 540  Nov 10 15:10 prop
(a) Type of file
(b) File permissions
(c) No. of links
(d) Owner of the file
(e) Group to which the file belongs
(f) Size of the file
(g) Date & time of last modification
(h) The name of the file
```

Some of the above need a little explanation. Once you have understood what each of the above mean, we will see how to edit the file **"prop"**.

(a) Type of file

You will recall that we had discussed the file types in the previous chapters. To recapitulate, a file can be ordinary text file, or a directory, or a special file. (Got it!) Now type

```
$ ls-l                          <Ret>
                 - {No file name has been specified}
 drwxr—r— 1 hans class 100 Nov 1 10:10 cust
 -rwx— — — 1 hans class 540 Nov 1 10:10 prop
$
```

{ (-) means ordinary file & "d" means directory file.}

The next nine characters can be divided into three units of three characters each. The first unit represents the owner of the file. The second unit represents the group and the third unit represents others. You will observe that each unit has three characters viz., r,w,x which stand for read, write & execute respectively. Are you feeling lost? Don't panic. The nine characters of the file type can be shown as follows

```
OWNER          GROUP      OTHERS
r w x          r w x      r w x
|                |            |
read            write       execute
```

Fig 4.3

In a typical office environment you can be the **'owner'** of the file and belong to the **'group'** of programmers while the **'others'** will be your colleagues from other departments.

In Fig 4.3, you as the owner have the permission to read the file, write on the file & execute it. The group members and others also have the same privileges. More about this when we look at subsequent commands.

Hans This is the name of the owner of the file. It is possible that there are files in your directory which you do not own (surprised!).

Class This is the name of the group to which the owner belongs.

540 Nov 10 15:0 The size of the file is given in bytes.

Date & Time The date and time that the file was last modified.

prop The name of the file. Having understood the meaning of each character of the output of {ls -l} let's get back to our original problem. The editing of the file **'prop'.** In order to be able to edit a given file you should have the permission to read and write to the file. Since you are in the same group as Hans is, the file permission should read as follows

```
-rwxrw-- -- 1 hans class 540 --
```

Let us see what the permission elements indicate for the file **'prop'.** Type

```
$ ls -l prop                  <Ret>
  -rwx-- -- -- 1 hans class 540 nov 10 15:10 prop
```

Elements from fifth to tenth are '-' which means that both the group members and 'others' do not have the privilege to read or write to the file or to execute the file. We can't possibly let Hans down, by not vetting his proposal, can we? There are two ways out of this situation.

(a) we should know the password of Hans and login as Hans.

(b) change the permission or file attributes of the file **'prop'**.

NOTE: We can change the permission of a file only if we are the owner of the file or if we login as the super user (system administrator).

So we call Hans, get the password from him and login as Hans. Right on. Let's go about first changing the permission of the file and then you can copy the file to your own directory and edit it.

4.16.1

chmod **change file permissions**
[chmod (+/-rwx) {file name}]
[chmod nnn {file name}]

Before we begin changing the mode of a file, it is a good idea to see the present mode of the file. Type

```
$ ls -l prop                <Ret>
  -rwx– – –  1 hans class 540 nov 10 15:10 prop.
```

In order to give read permission to group & others type

```
$ chmod +r  prop                <Ret>
$
```

Let us see what has happened to the file attributes. Type

(1)

```
$ ls -l prop              <Ret>
  -rwxr–r–  1 hans class 540 nov 10 15:10 prop
$
```

To give the write permission only to the group type

(2)

```
$ chmod g+w prop              <Ret>
$
```

Now type

```
$ ls-l prop              <Ret>
  -rwxrw–r–  1 hans class 540 nov 10 15:10 prop
$
```

Have you observed the difference between (1) & (2). What is it? You can view the file now using the page command.

We have so far been giving away privileges to all and sundry. How do we revoke those privileges? Just a little while ago we had given a read privilege to **'others'**. Let us revoke this privilege, type

```
$ chmod o-r prop            <Ret>
$
```

To see the result of the above, type

```
$ ls-l prop                  <Ret>
-rwxrw– –  1 hans class 540 nov 10 15:10 prop
```

How do we revoke the read & write permission for the group with just one command? Type

```
$ chmod g-rw prop        <Ret>
$ ls-l prop
  -rwx---  1 hans class 540 nov 10 15:10 prop
$
```

There ! You have done it.

But wait! Is it not rather tedious to type in the option one by one when we can specify the same thing using numbers? Here's how! First let us again focus our attention at the nine elements that denote the availabiliity of file access privileges or otherwise.

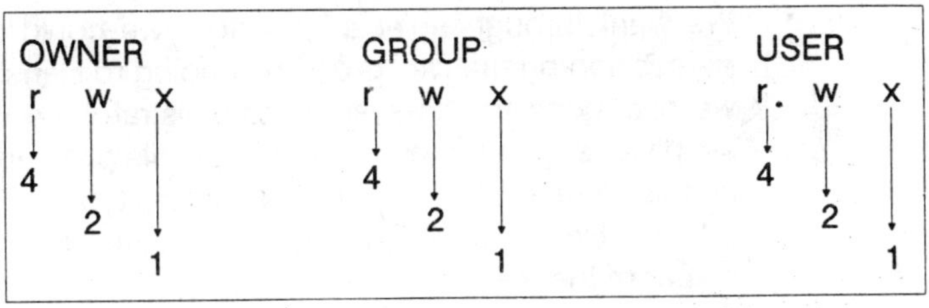

Fig. 4.4

Observe, that for each **'r'** you have a value of 4, for each **'w'** you have a value of 2 & for each **'x'** you have a value of 1. If you total (r+w+x) for each group you get the value 7 for each group. Let us work through an example and it will become clearer.

Recall that the file **'prop'** has **r,w** & **x** permission for the owner only. Suppose we wanted to grant read write permission to the group and **'x'** (execute) permission to others, then type

```
$ chmod 761 prop            <Ret>
        | | |
        | | Permission to others
        | Permission for group
        Permission for user
```

If you want to give only execute permission to the group and others then type

```
$ chmod 711 prop        <Ret>
$
```

Check the permission and see for yourself.

Ofcourse, now you want to edit the file prop right? But what is the hurry? You have not been introduced to the editor yet. Wait till you learn to edit. Then you can do a better job, for your enthusiasm will be aided by knowledge.

4.16.2

chown **change file ownership**

[chown (new owner) {file name}]

We went through quiet a lot before we could change the permission on the file **"prop"** belonging to Hans. Actually if we had gone to the system administrator he would have simply changed the ownership of the file prop and saved us all this trouble. He would have simply typed the following or then Hans could have done the same since he is the owner of the file.

```
$ chown mohan prop        <Ret>
$
```

Now mohan is the new owner of the file. Type

```
$ ls -l prop                <Ret>
  -rwx— — — 1 mohan class 540 Nov 10 15:10 prop
$
```

4.16.3

chgrp **change group of file**

[chgrp (new group) {File name}]

Similarly you can change the group to which the file belongs. By doing this, the current group becomes **'others'.** Type

```
$ chgrp klass prop          <Ret>
$
```

Now see the file attributes, type

```
$ ls -l prop                    <Ret>
  -rwxrwx--- 1 mohan klass 540 Nov 10 15:10 prop
$
```

We have had a look at file security and seen how the UNIX system can restrict access to your files if you want to keep some files away from the public.

4.17

passwd

change user password
[passwd]

Just as we have changed the owner of the file, the group to which the file belongs etc, we can change our password too. Now that Hans' password is known to us (Remember we logged in as Hans to vet the prop file ?) he would like to change his password to a new one. And this is how he would do it

```
$ passwd                    <Ret>
  enter password (********)
$
```

The system will ask Hans to enter the new password twice in order to reconfirm. In some implementations of UNIX the system will ask for the current password before prompting you to enter the new password.

It is always a good practice to change your password regularly in order to avoid unauthorised access.

On this note we will conclude this chapter. Let us take a re-look at the commands discussed so far.

write	Send a message to another user who has logged on.
mesg y	Allow other users to communicate with you
mail	Send a message to another user. The receiver need not be logged on.
find	To locate a file
head n	To view first n lines of a file.

tail n	To view last n lines of a file.
more	To view a file page by page
sort	To sort the records of a file based on a key(s)
grep	search for a string in a file(s).
cut	display selected fields.
tr	squeeze extra space between two fields.
uniq	display unique records in a file.
comm	list common and unique records between two files.
cmp	display the first character where two files vary.
chmod	Change file permissions
chown	Change ownership of file.
chgrp	Change group to which a file belongs.
passwd	Assign/Change password.

We have so far seen more than thirty commands under UNIX. There are many, many more commands under UNIX. Some of them we will discuss in subsequent chapters. With this repertoire of commands (limited though it may seem when comparead to the total number of commands under UNIX) you will be able to perform all the tasks required of you as an user of an UNIX box.

Now complete the exercise and go on to the next chapter.

EXERCISE

Attempt all questions without referring to the book.

1. Find out how many users are presently logged?
2. Send a message to one of the users. Interrupt his work.
3. Give necessary commands to prevent the users from disturbing you
4. Send a message to another user without disturbing him
5. Create a file "poem" using cat. The contents should be the rhyme 'Ding Dong Bell – -'
6. Count the no. of words & character in the file
7. Display the first two lines and the last two lines of the file 'poem'.
8. Create two files with a list of names in each. Print out the names common to both the files.
9. What is the difference between "comm", "cmp" and "uniq".
10. Find all files with names starting with "k". Search from the /usr directory.
12. Find all files not newer than /test1 in the /usr directory.
13. How will you see the contents of a file from the 15th line onwards.
14. How will you get a file which has the word "Hundred" in it?
15. How will you display the first and fourth fields of the file "test1". Assume that more than one blank spaces separate each field.
16. Display the user name and home directory of all users.
17. Create a file and give only execute permission to your group members and others.
18. Create another file and give all permissions only for "others".
19. Create a file and change the ownership. Then change its permissions.
20. Find and delete all files with the word "good".
21. How will you delete all files with the names starting with "k".

22. Create a file called 'item' with the following fields

item code	Alpha numeric
items	Alpha
supplier code	Numeric
rate/unit	Numeric
quantity on hand	Numeric
value	Numeric

Think of and enter atleast 10 to 15 items. The field separator must be ':'.

23. Display all the items whose supplier code is 1.

24. Display all the items where quantity on hand is 10.

25. Sort the file 'item' in order of increasing rate.

26. Sort the file 'item' on item code within supplier's code.

27. Display item code, q.o.h & value for all items supplied by S2.

28. Display all items with item name starting with 'B'.

5

vi EDITOR

Having learnt the operating system commands, you would now like to write or create shell scripts, write program in "C" or COBOL, create documents, send mail etc. Remember, we were supposed to vet a proposal by Hans? In order to do so you will need to know how to view a file using an editor, how to move around the screen, how to insert, delete text etc.

The "vi" editor is perhaps the most powerful & user friendly editors available under UNIX today. In order to demonstrate the various features of "vi", we will take a small file (i.e.) games to work on. We will take the "vi" session in the following stages.

(i) Basic "vi"
(ii) Advanced "vi"

Basic "vi"

Entering vi. It is very simple. Simply type:

```
$ vi games
  |F|ootball
  Hockey
  Cricket
  Tennis
  Squash
  Polo
  ~
  "games" 6 lines, 37 characters
```

NOTE

* The box (| |) denotes the cursor.
* "games" is the file name, with 6 lines & 37 characters.
* ~ in the first column means an unwritten line without text (NOT A BLANK LINE).
* The box has been drawn arbitrarily to show what the screen will look like.

5.0

moving around Before we begin to change the text or add text we should be able to move around the screen. In some cases you can use the arrow keys. However, if the "vi" editor that you have, does not support this, you should use the following keys

k [UP]
h [LEFT]
l [RIGHT]
j [DOWN]

using the above keys you can move all over the screen. Let us see how it is done. You change from the "insert" or "append" mode to the command mode by pressing the "esc" key. To perform any activity, be it, mostly moving around or deleting words or characters you must first press the "esc" key.

```
Football
Hockey
Cricket
Tennis
Squash
Polo
~
~
"games" 6 lines, 37 char
```

l
move
right

```
Football
Hockey
Cricket
Tennis
squash
Polo
~
~
"games" 6 lines, 37 char
```

```
F ootball
Hockey
Cricket
Tennis
Squash
Polo
~
~
"games" 6 lines, 37 char
```

3 l
move
right 3

```
Foot ball
Hockey
Cricket
Tennis
squash
Polo
~
~
"games" 6 lines, 37 char
```

If "h" is used instead of "l" as above, the cursor will move to the left. If "j" is used, the cursor will move down and if k is used the cursor will move up.

However if you use "k" now, when the curosr is placed in the first line the system will voice its displeasure with a "beep". Similarly you cannot use "l" at the end of a line, "h" at the beginning of a line and "j" at the end of the file or the last line of the file.

l → To move cursor one column to right of current position
h→ To move cursor one column to left of curent position
k→ To move cursor one line above the current line.
j → To move cursor one line below the current line.

modes

The "vi" operates in two modes, namely

→ Insert or append mode
→ command mode

insert and append

To enter into insert mode type "i" followed by the text you want to insert.

Before		After
Football Hockey Cricket Tennis Squash Polo ~ ~ "games" 6 lines, 37 char	"i" lute insert text →	lute Football Hockey Cricket Tennis squash Polo ~ ~ "games" 6 lines, 41 char

Before After

Observe that the cursor is still on "F"

lute Football Hockey Cricket Tennis Squash Polo ~ ~ "games" 6 lines, 41 char	a lute append text →	lute Flute o otball Hockey Cricket Tennis squash Polo ~ ~ "games" 6 lines, 45 char

Observe that the cursor is now on "o".

In the case of insert (i) the text is inserted before the character on which the cursor is positioned.

Append (a) inserts the text after the character on which the cursor is positioned. Although we have added text in the above cases, the number of characters is still 37 this is because we have not saved the file and reopened it.

Leaving "vi"

luteFluteootball Hockey Cricket Tennis Squash Polo ~ ~ "games" 6 lines, 37 char	Esc:q!	Football Hockey Cricket Tennis squash Polo ~ ~ "games" 6 lines, 37 char

To come out of insert mode or append mode press ESC. This will put you in command mode. Now you can use any of the various text, cursor manipulation commands. To save the file and to come out of vi you can press "ZZ" (two capital Z's). But sometimes you may not want to save the changes you have just made or you may want to save the file but to continue to work on it. TABLE IB gives you the options to save & quit.

COMMAND	FUNCTION
ESC : q!	quit without saving
ESC : q	quit without saving
ESC : w	write to the file & continue
ESC : x	save & quit
ESC zz	save & quit

TABLE 5.1

deleting a character

You delete a character by positioning the cursor on it and pressing "x". The character gets deleted and the line moves one character to the left. If you continue to press "x", then the entire line to its left gets deleted. Of course when the cursor reaches the beginning of the line and you still continue to press "x" then the system will "beep". As in the case of l,k,h,j you can use a number to specify how many character you want deleted.

deleting a word

"vi" recognises words as a group of characters separated by space, punctuation marks or tabs. To delete a word, place the cursor on the first character of the word & press "dw" (delete word).

In this session we have covered the basics of "vi" that are given in the TABLE 5.2

COMMAND	FUNCTION
l	→ Move cursor right
k	^ Move cursor up
h	← Move cursor left
j	Move cursor down
i	insert text (before cursor)
a	insert text (after cursor)
dw	delete a word
x	delete character
+	the save & quit options

TABLE 5.2

Now to go on to the Advanced vi options. In this phase the options will be presented to you at a quick pace. It is expected that you are more familiar with the commands given in the first phase. You should know by now, that while attempting any manipulation of text you should be in the COMMAND MODE.

You came to the COMMAND MODE by pressing ESC. Got it!! Here we go!

Deleting a line If all words, characters of a line are deleted, that space is not taken up by the line following it. We have to explicitly delete the line. To do this press "dd". The line where the cursor is presently positioned gets deleted.

undo You may by mistake type "5 d" i.e. delete five lines and belatedly realise that you only wanted to delete two lines. One alternative is to retype the three lines that you have deleted by mistake. Alternately when you press "Esc u" the five lines that had disappeared from the face of the terminal will reappear. The "u" will help you "undo" what has been done by the last command.

scrolling In the first phase we saw that we could move the cursor up or down the screen and that we could also specify the number of lines by which the cursor should move. For example, you could type "Esc6j" for the cursor to move down six lines. Here the cursor would move down with the text being fixed. But if you want the text to move up or down with the cursor being at a fixed location you can use the following commands.

^U(Ctrl capital "U") -to scroll up 1/2 screen.
^D(Ctrl capital "D") -to scroll down 1/2 screen.

cursor movements on words Let us do some more work on words. To move forward by one word ie.to the first character of the next word press 'w'. To go to the end of the same word press 'e'. To go to the previous word (ie.) go back by one word press 'b'.

Now do not get confused by the following illustration. Here for one display three cursors have been used to show the difference between the three commands.

BEFORE		AFTER
This is an example to show cursor movement "new", 8 words, 35 char	w e b	This is an example to show cursor movement "new", 8 words, 35 char

move cursor to the end/beginning of line To move the cursor from any position on a line to the end of the line press '$'. To move the cursor from any position on the line to the first column of the line press '0' (zero).

create new line To create a new line between existing lines, press 'o' (oh!). A small 'o' creates a new line below the current line. A capital 'O' creates a new line above the current line.

replacing a character To replace a character place the cursor on the character that you want to replace and press 'r' then type the new character.

This is an example to show curser movement "new", 8 words, 35 cha	ro	This is an example to show cursor movement "new", 8 words, 35 char

search & replace

T his is an example to show cursor movement "new", 8 words, 35 cha	/s/is/was	This was an example to show cursor movement "new", 8 words, 35 char

string search If you want to locate a word or a string in a given text you can do so. Here's how!

Football Hockey Cricket Tennis Squash Polo ~ ~ "games", 6 lines, 37 chr	/Cric	Football Hockey Cricket Tennis Squash Polo ~ ~ "games", 6 lines, 37 chr

Observe that the cursor has jumped to the third line "Cricket". If you want to look for the next occurence of

"Cric" press "n". If you want to look at the previous occurence of "Cric" press "N".

numbering When, for example a "C" program code is submitted for compilation, you may get a message saying that a certain line number has an error of syntax. In situations like this you would no doubt like to see a display of your program code with each line numbered. In order to number the lines of a file type ":set nu".

Before		After
Football Hockey Cricket Tennis Squash Polo ~ ~ "games", 6 lines, 37 chr	:set nu	1 Football 2 Hockey 3 Cricket 4 Tennis 5 Squash 6 Polo ~ ~ "games", 6 lines, 37 chr

cursor jumping If you want to position your cursor at any given line for e.g. if you want to jump from the bottom of the file to the top then:-

Before		After
Football Hockey Cricket Tennis Squash Polo ~ ~ "games", 6 lines, 37 chr	:1	Football Hockey Cricket Tennis Squash Polo ~ ~ "games", 6 lines, 37 chr

cut & paste Often you have to yank out a line from one part of the text and introduce it into another part of the text where you feel its more appropriate. This process will have to be done in two steps.

(1) to yank out or cut the line(s) and

(2) to insert the yanked line(s).

Step 1

an example to demonstrate the cut and paste steps This is ~ "new1", 10 owrds, 37 char	yy	an example to demonstrate the cut and paste steps ~ "new1", 10 owrds, 37 char

Step 2 Move the cursor to the line where you want to paste the line.

an example to demonstrate the cut and paste steps ~ "new1", 10 owrds, 37 char	^ p	This is an example to demonstrate the cut and paste steps ~ "new1", 10 owrds, 37 char

Conclusion What has been covered so far is by no means the complete repertoire of 'vi" commands. Nor has this text attempted to do so. However if you are thorough with what has been covered so far you will be able to handle all your day to day editing requirements.

TABLE 5.3 gives you a command summary for "vi"

COMMAND SUMMARY

COMMAND	FUNCTION
l	move cursor right
h	move cursor left
k	move cursor up by one line
j	move cursor one line below
i	insert text (before cursor)
a	append text (after cursor)
x	delete character
dd	delete line
dw	delete word
r	replace text
u	undo last change
:10	goto line number 10
set: nu	set line numbers
/get	search for string "get"
n	next occurence of pattern
N	previous occurence of pattern
/s/get/got	replace "get" with "got"

COMMAND	FUNCTION
^D	scroll down 1/2 page
^U	scroll up 1/2 page
$	go to end of line
0 (zero)	go to beginning of line
o (oh !)	create blank line below current line
O (oh!)	create blank line above current line
:q!	quit without saving
:w	save and continue
:wq	save and quit
:x	save and quit
zz	save and quit

TABLE 5:3

Invest a little time and effort on "vi" or for that matter on any of the editors that you like. This will save you considerable time and frustration when you begin to write shell scripts or programs on any other language. Now go through the following exercise. Remember the more you work on the editor the better you get.

EXERCISE

1. What are the two modes that the vi works in?
2. How do you enter a character in an existing file ?
3. What is the first key that you will press as you begin creating a new file using vi?
4. What does "3 l" do? When will this not work?
5. How will you delete a word?
6. When will you use this sequence [Esc:cw] ?
7. What are the various ways to save a file ?
8. What is the command tog to the end of a line ?
9. How will you set line numbers ?
10. Without quitting from the editor how will you run an Unix command ?
11. Cut and paste two lines from the end of a file to the middle of a file.
12. Copy two lines from the beginning of a file to the end of the file.
13. How will you insert a blank line ?
14. How will you delete a blank line ?

6

SHELL PROGRAMMING

In the chapters "Getting Started with Unix I & II", we have seen a host of commands. We saw commands to create a file, read a file, search a file, to see all the users who have logged on to the system and so forth. We simply typed in our commands at the $ prompt, pressed the ENTER key and expected the Unix system to respond with the appropriate answer. We know for a fact that the Shell interprets our command and presents it to the kernel and reconverts the kernel output and presents it to us in a form we understand. But the shell does more than just play interpretor. It performs a host of functions. Let us examine them one by one, before we go on to programming the shell.

6.1 Functions of shell

Following are the functions performed by the shell.

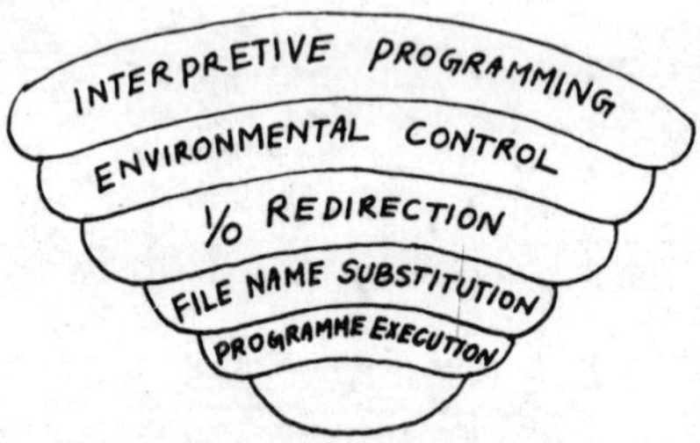

FUNCTIONS OF SHELL

6.1.1 Program execution

Recall our discussion on shell in the chapter Structure of Unix. As has been mentioned, the shell interprets anything we type against the $ prompt. The line on which we type the command is called the "command line". The shell treats the first word (A word is a set of characters ending with a space) as the command and the following characters as the arguments of the command.

For example

```
$ mv birds feathers        <Ret>
```

"mv" is the command and "birds" & "feathers" are the arguments. The shell ensures that the arguments are correctly handed over to the command for execution. Once the command is executed, the shell takes control again and communicates with the user in the manner dictated by the command. In this case the shell will simply display the $ prompt.

6.1.2

file name substitution

In the previous chapters we were introduced to the wild card characters like "?", "*", "[]". The onus is on the shell to interpret the meaning of the wild card characters and substitute the same. If you had files likes games1, games2, gamesx, gamesxy, gamesabc then a command as follows

```
$ cat games?                <Ret>
```

will be interpreted as

```
$ cat games1 games2 gamesx  <Ret>
```

and a command

```
$ cat ga*  <Ret>
```

will be interpretted as

```
$ cat games games1 games2 gamesx gamesxy
gamesabc  <Ret>
```

the ? means any one character
* means any no. of characters
[] lets you represent a restricted range of single character {e.q} [a-e] means "a" to "e".

6.1.3

I/O redirection

If a command is given thus

```
$ cat birds  > beaks        <Ret>
```

the shell opens a file 'beaks' and connects the output of "cat birds" to the file beaks. This file treats the output of "cat birds" as standard input.

6.1.4

pipe line hookup When pipes are used, between two commands, the first command does not have to worry about where its output goes. At the same time the second program is not concerned about the source of its input. This transparent hookup is the responsibility of the shell.

6.1.5

Environment control The shell lets you build your own "environment" right from the $ prompt sign to the commands that you type. E.g. "cp" can be called "copy", "ls" can be called 'list'. How this is done, we will see soon enough.

6.1.6

Interpretive programming language The shell itself is a powerful language. You can directly write loop construct in the shell language and execute them or you can save them in a file and execute them.

6.2

VARIABLES An important aspect of a programming language is the use of variables. Variables are used to pass values to a program and change the parameters where necessary.

6.2.1

Shell variable The shell also allows you to define variables. A variable name can begin with any letter or underscore and can have a total of more than one character. But we must always have only meaningful names for variables.

6.2.1 a

How to assign value to variables

```
$ name=kumar          <Ret>
$
```

The value "kumar" is assigned to the variable 'name'. No spaces should be there between the variable name, = and the value assigned.

```
$ name=Ram kumar     <Ret>
$
```

This is incorrect. If there is a space between the value or if the value is a string with spaces in between, enclose the string in quotes like

```
$ name = "Ram kumar"    < Ret >
$
```

The variable in a shell does not have any "type". The value assigned to a variable is treated as a string.

6.2.1b

To display the value of variable

The variable is assigned a value for use in a program for computation or to display the same. To display the value of a variable say "name", type

```
$ echo $ name                 < Ret >
  Ram kumar
$
```

[Remember echo $HOME?]

When the "echo" command encounters a "$" sign followed by a variable name, it displays the contents of the variable at that point. For e.g.

```
$ echo My name is $name              < Ret >
  My name is Ram kumar
$
```

If, on the other hand you type

```
$ echo My name is $name1             < Ret >
  My name is
$
```

If a variable is used that has not been assigned a value so far, you will not get any display. This is known as 'null'value.

We will look at one useful example of assigning value to variables. If you were to frequently copy files from a directory say /usr/train/mohan/unix to another directory say /usr/bus/ananth/oracle then this is what you do. Type

```
$ S=/usr/train/mohan/unix          <Ret>
$ d=/usr/bus/ananth/oracle         <Ret>
$ cp $S/one  $d                    <Ret>
$
```

(Where "one" is the file to be copied) As simple as that!

6.3

sh: We have just seen how it is possible to use value assignment to variables and how it can save us a lot of typing and time.

Suppose we want the system to greet the user and display the date and time, this is what you should do

```
$ cat  > greet              <Ret>
echo "WELCOME TO KLASS COMPUTERS"
echo "Today's date and current time is"
date  "Ctrl d"
```

Next we supply the file name as an argument to "sh" as follows

```
$ sh greet  <Ret>
  WELCOME TO KLASS COMPUTERS
  Today's date and current time is
  Mon Nov 12 07:30  Ist 1991
$
```

The "sh" command creates a new subshell which takes up the execution of the file "greet". Each line in the file "greet" is executed. Once the subshell completes the execution of the file "greet" it expires and the control is handed back to the parent shell. Any number of subshells can be invoked by a program.

6.2.1c

exporting variables As we know now, one shell can invoke a child shell process which in turn can invoke another child shell and so on. But what about the variables. How are they treated between shells? Let us see.

```
$ name= Mohan                    <Ret>
              [At first shell, name gets the value  Mohan]
$ echo $ name Mohan
$ sh
              [Invoke child shell]
$ echo $ name      No response

$ name=Kumar
       [In the second shell, 'name' gets the value 'Kumar']
$ echo $ name Kumar
$ ^d          [Exit from child shell, go to parent shell]
$ echo $ name Mohan
$        The parent shell does not know about the value
         of 'name' which was assigned in the child process]
```

"New shell" or child shell means the same thing in relation to "old shell or parent shell".

If we want the new shell to know about all the variables assigned in the old shell, then we have to export the variables. This means the variables are made global for all subsequent subshells or child shells created thereafter. Let us repeat the previous example again, after exporting the variable"name".

```
$ export name             <Ret>
$ name=Mohan <Ret> (Mohan is the first value of
'name')
$ echo $ name
  Mohan
$ sh (Starting new shell)
$ echo $ name
  Mohan
$ name=Kumar
$ echo $ name
  Kumar
$ ^d (Return to parent shell)
$ echo $ name
  Mohan (Original value of 'name' is
                            unchanged)
$
```

When we export a variable, a copy of the variable is passed on to the shells created subsequently.

6.4

shell scripts

We have seen that a shell script is a command or sequence of commands stored in a file which is executed by typing

```
$ sh {filename}  <Ret>
```

The scripts we have seen so far are fairly primitive and definitely not interactive. A script should be interactive i.e it must prompt the user to enter the information needed, so that the user feels involved and can follow what is going on. Alternately the script should accept the arguments on the command line itself as the UNIX command usually does. E.g.,

```
$ cp a b <Ret>
   [copy file a to file b]
```

The second approach is faster of the two. But it will not make you popular with other users if you create shell scripts like the above for them. Let us create an interactive shell script. In this process you will be introduced to the **'read'** command. It does not need any special explanation.

```
$ cat > display <Ret>
   echo which file do you want to view\?
   read file
   more $file ('Ctrl d')
```

Convert the file **display** into an executable file (you should know how it is done) and type

```
$ display  <Ret>
   which file do you want to view?
   birds      <Ret>
   sparrow
   eagle
   parrot
   peacock
   kiwi
   100% birds
$
```

Have you observed the '\' before the question mark '?' in the program **"display"**. It is not there when the file is executed. Try and recall where we have mentioned the use of '\'.

6.5

positional parameters

You have now created a shell script which is interactive. What about the other approach of creating a script which is not verbose. Remember UNIX is not so communicativie. We should also create crisp scripts. Once again recall the discussion in chapter II on how the shell interprets the commands we type on the command line. The first word or character is treated as the command and the word following that are treated as arguments to the command. Let us give them a number

```
$ cp    kb    bk
  |     |     |
  $0    $1    $2
```

The command is always referred to as $0.
The arguments to the command are $1 $2 $3 etc.,
The total no. of arguments is $#
All the arguments will be displayed by $*

In the case of

```
$ cp kb bk                    <Ret>
$0 = cp
$1 = kb
$2 = bk
$# = 2
$* = kb bk
```

You are not fully sure how we got the abcve. Take a look at this

```
$ cat>Posish                  <Ret>
  echo This is to demonstrate $0-nal parameters
  echo The arguments are $*
  echo There are a total of $# arguments
  echo The second argument is $2
  echo The third argument is $3
  echo I hope you have got it (Ctrl d)
```

```
$ sh posish command line arguments      <Ret>
  This is to demonstrate posish-nal parameters
  The arguments are: command line arguments
  There are a total of 3 arguments
  The second argument is: line
  The third argument is: arguments
  I hope you have got it
$
```

Let us work out an example. Suppose you had a subdirectory whose full path name is **/usr/train/mohan/unix.** If your friend wanted to copy some files to your directory from another directory say **/usr/bus/gopal.**

If the file to be copied is **"gopal"** and the file should have a secondary name gp, then he can do the following

```
$ cat Copy                    <Ret>
  cp $1 /usr/train/mohan/unix/$1.gp
  echo file copied to $1.gp ("Ctrl d")
$
```

```
$ copy gopal                  <Ret>
  file copied to gopal.gp
$
```

This is what happened.

(1) In the command **{copy gopal}** the file gopal is considered as $1

(2) The file copy instructs that $1 (e.g) **"gopal"** be copied to **/usr/train/mohan/unix** directory under the name $1.gp (e.g) **gopal.gp**

(3) It then displays a message that the file has been copied.

6.6

set

The **"set"** command is part of the shell and is used very effectively for command substitution. If a particular command is enclosed in back quotes ['] in conjunction with **echo,** the **echo** command will display the output of the enclosed command.

```
$ echo who                    <Ret>
  who
$ echo 'who'                  <Ret>
  mohan  tty03  Nov 10 9:15
  ramesh tty0  Nov 10 9:00
$
```

Now if we type

```
$ set 'date'                  <Ret>
$ echo $1                     <Ret>
  Mon
$
```

This is what happened:

The 'date' command gets executed as
Mon Nov 10 09:30:31 Ist 1991
and the shell reads it as
$ set Mon Nov 10 09:30:31 Ist 1991
So $1 is Mon

Let us work out one more example.

Suppose you are asked to create a general script that will help the user to add his name as the secondary name of all his files. What would you do?
The function of the script is two fold.
*** It must obtain the name of the user.
*** It must rename the file with the name obtained in the format (filename.username) This is what you do

```
$ cat seal               <Ret>
file=$1 (This $1 is the argument given by the user
              (e.g) the  file to be renamed)
set 'who am i' (This will execute "who am i" so each
              user will have his name as $1).
mv $file $file.$1 ("Ctrl d")
$
```

Let us try

```
$ ls                <Ret>
  birds
  feathers
  games
  games1
  bk
  kb
Seal
$
```

If the user name is mohan, then

```
$ seal bk              <Ret>
$
```

Check the directory again

```
$ ls                <Ret>
  birds
  feathers
  games
  games 1
  bk.mohan
  kb
  seal
$
```

Explanation: Here, in the command **"seal bk"**. $1 = bk and the value "bk" was assigned to "file" [file = $1]. Next we said "set 'who am i' ". This gave the value "mohan tty 03 Nov 10 09:15 "and now $1 is **"mohan"**. So, mv $file $file.$1 will be read as

```
mv bk bk.mohan
```

We will leave **"set"** now and look at some shell variables

6.7 system shell variables

Apart from the variables we create, (i.e) local and global the shell has its own set of shell variables. These variables and their contents are as follows.

VARIABLE	VALUE
HOME	The users home directory
PATH	Full pathname of directories that are to be searched for programs executed as commands.
MAIL	Filename of the user's mailbox
PS1	Shell prompt character or string (default $)
PS2	Secondary prompt when further input is required
MAIL CHECK	Frequency of checks to be made with regard to mail received by MAIL

You will recall that we had mentioned the facilities provided by the UNIX system, which will help you build a unique interface between the user and the O/S. We have seen how you can build your own little library of commands that are more informative and meaningful than the rather cryptic commands of UNIX. Depending upon the user, you can create an environment which is most ideal for him. The above variables help you build the environment. We will briefly discuss each of the above variables and later on look at the **"Profile"** file in which the environment parameters are stored.

6.7.1

HOME

In the chapter Getting Started with UNIX-I, after logging in you typed

```
$ pwd
  /usr/train
$
```

The system displayed your 'current working directory'. Now having done so much work on your system, if after logging in you type **"pwd"** you would still get the same message **"/usr/train".** But during the course of your work, you would be jumping from one directory to another. Your pwd may change but your HOME directory will be the same. Let us see. Type:

```
$ echo $HOME
  /usr/train
$
```

Now type

```
$ cd /usr/bus/unix      <Ret>
$ pwd                   <Ret>
  /usr/bus/unix
$ echo $HOME            <Ret>
  /usr/train
$
```

The **/usr/train** is your login directory or HOME directory. Let us confirm. Go to the root directory and type

```
$ vi /etc/passwd  <Ret>
          (output will consist of lines like this)
mohan: 7e%i9:2:7:mohankumar:/usr/train:/bin/sh
user's                              program to be
name                                executed at login

user's                   home
encrypted               directory
pass word          user's
                   full name
user's no
          group no.
```

This has been discussed in the chapter Structure of UNIX.

The HOME directory is the directory to which you are set as soon as you login. When you login and give your password the system reads the **/etc/passwd** file to check if the password is correct and also reads your HOME directory and ensures that you are correctly placed. And the program that has to be executed on logging in is duly executed.

The value of HOME is used by the command 'cd' when it is given without any arguments.

6.7.2

PATH While the environment created for a user is to let him feel comfortable. It can also be used by the super user to impose restrictions on the user.

The PATH contains the absolute pathnames of all the directories that can be accessed by the user. If you type

```
$ echo $PATH          <Ret>
   .: /usr/oracle:/usr/train:/bin
$
```

This means that when you give a command e.g. **"cp a b"**, the system will first search through **/usr/oracle** for the command **'cp'.** If the search is not successful it will search through **/usr/train** and again if it is not successful, it will go through **/bin**. If the command **'cp'** exists it will execute the command or it will respond by displaying the message 'command not found'. If the super user does not want to give the user the privilege to copy or remove files, he can simply remove the **'cp'** & **'mv'** command from the directories mentioned in the user's PATH.

Alternatively, you can include the little library of commands that you have built up into the directories of your PATH and work in an environment that you like.

6.7.3

MAIL This has been discussed in the chapter Getting Started with UNIX- II.

6.7.4

PS1 The default prompt is $. If you do not like this, you can change it to 'MOHAN' by typing

```
$ PS1 = 'MOHAN' <Ret> (change prompt to MOHAN)
MOHAN pwd <Ret> (prompt has been changed)
/usr/train
MOHAN
```

To change the prompt back to $, type

```
MOHAN PS1 ='$' <Ret>
$
```

6.7.5

PS2 In case you want to change the secondary prompt follow the steps with PS2 as you did with PS1.

6.7.6

MAIL CHECK You can specify the interval in seconds after which the system should check the MAIL to see if any new mail has arrived. If some new mail has arrived, it will notify the user.

In the past couple of pages we have been talking of variables. There is a lot more of this heavy stuff in the form of 'special shell variables', 'escape mechanisms', 'command terminators', 'redirection' etc.,

In the above concepts will be introduced to you as we go ahead with writing shell programs. Shell programming is primarily using the commands that you have learnt so far (some more will be introduced to you) to perform some of the day to day function. Right HO! Then cn to shell programming.

shell scripts

Before we begin writing a shell script or a shell program it is good idea to analyse the reason for choosing the shell script method over the use of conventional languages. First we must understand the problem and then see if we can use the existing utilities and write a script which will solve the problem. The UNIX 'C' philosophy is to build on the work done by others. This philosophy is sensible too. After all what is the sanctity in reinventing the wheel? So if we alreay have some utilities to do a job or a set of utilities which can to do the job let us use them to solve our problem. For example, observe the following 'C' program.

```
main ()
{
  int i ;
  for (i=0; i <=24; i++)
printf (\n);
}
```

This program helps you clear the screen. Instead of using 'C' to write this program we can use the UNIX utility {"tput clear"} which also clears the screen. Well, you know which of the two you will use.

All the programs written will have any or all of these fundamental functions.

**** Read/Write a file
**** Compare & Compute
**** Check for a condition to execute

As you proceed now, you will be introduced to commands that will accept data from the terminal (read), then we will talk of arithmetic operations and options for numerical comparisons.

We will start with loop constructs.

6.8

loop constructs You normally come across situations where you want to do a thing till a certain point of time & also you would like not to do a thing upto a point of time. So the execution of activity depends upon a condition.

E.g., You sleep till it is 5:30 A.M. Now you can break your sleep on two conditions.

(1) You wake up because your body has had enough sleep/rest (INTERNAL)
or

(2) An alarm goes off breaking your sleep (EXTERNAL)

We will study loop constructs which depend on external inputs or for something to happen from within.

6.8.1

the 'if' statement Syntax

```
if condition
then
   commands
fi
```

Open a file and enter the following text.

```
if [$1 = mohan]
  then
        echo "Good morning $1"
fi
```

Change the file into an executable file and run it. If the file name is **'one',** then

```
$ one mohan
  Good Morning Mohan
$
```

But if you type

```
$ one gopal
$
```

The script **'one'** checks if the value of $1 is equal to **'mohan'.** In the first case the condition was TRUE (i.e.) $1 was Mohan and then it executed the (echo "Good morning $1") statement. In the second case the value of $1 was not Mohan, so it skipped the command (echo "Good morning $")

NOTE: *The 'if' statement in the UNIX command language does not look directly for the value of a variable, but it looks to see if the 'if' command is successful. You will appreciate this better as we work on more examples.*

6.8.2

if : else

The above example that we worked out was rather tame, especially when we expect so much more from UNIX. Let us give some pep to the above script. Make the changes that will make the program look like:

```
if [ $1 = mohan ]
  then
         echo "Good day to you $1"
         echo "There is a message for you"
         more message
  else
         echo "You are not supposed to use this
                 directory $1, beat it!"
fi
```

Here, we saw the inclusion of the **'else'** bit which controls the execution of the program thus

```
if [condition]
  then
           commands}     DO IF TRUE
           commands}
  else
           commands}     DO IF NOT TRUE
           commands}
fi
```

6.8.3

elif

The two **'if'** constructs you have seen so far perform a particular job if the condition is true and perform another job if it is false. But all our jobs are not so simple, they are much more complicated. Let us look at the following example.

You have given a command **{ mv kb cd }** and the contents of PATH are

```
$ echo $ PATH
.:/bin:/usr/bin:/usr/train:
$
```

Now the UNIX system will scan through the current directory denoted by (.). If the command is not found there, it will scan through **/bin** directory. If the command **'mv'** is not found here also it will scan the **/usr/bin** directory and so forth till it finds the **'mv'** command. If the command is not found in any of the directories, it will display the message "command not found".

Let us try out a program first using the above directories as the directories to be searched. Create a script as follows. Call the script **"fserch"**

```
echo enter the name of the file to search
read file
find / -name $file -print > kl
if grep /usr/mohan/$file kl
  then
            echo File $file found in /usr/mohan
elif grep /bin/$file kl
  then
            echo File $file found in /bin
elif grep /usr/bin/ $file kl
  then
            echo File $file found in /usr/bin
elif grep /usr/train/$file kl
  then
            echo File $ file found in /usr/train
else
            echo file not found
fi
```

Have you noticed the construct above? A new keyword **'elif'** has been introduced. The **'elif'** actually is a sort of acronym for **'else if'.** You use **'elif'** if there are a number of **'ifs'** in a construct. Each **'elif'** should have its own 'control condition' and commands to be carried out on the **'elif'** being true. The last **'elif'** must have its ending with the **'else'** and **'fi'.** Following is the syntax.

```
if control condition -1
  then
            command -1
elif control condition -2
  then
            command -2
elif control condition -3
  then
            command -3
.
.
.
.
else
  then
            default
fi
```

We have so far seen three types of **'if'** constructs. The **'elif'** construct providing the maximum flexibility.

The above constructs check for a condition and execute the commands therein. The program executes once and then terminates. If on the contrary you want the program to execute for a specified number of times then the above constructs will be of little help. So let us look at some other constructs which help us to write scripts that can be executed for a specified number of times.

6.9 'for' loop

A loop as you know is a formation that goes round & round on the same path. In programming environment, looping is used to make a program execute the same steps for a specified number of times. Among the 'loop' constructs we have **'for', 'while'** & **'until'.** We will first look at the 'for' loop. Following is the syntax.

```
for [variable name ] in [ value(s) ]
do
  commands
done
```

Recall the 'C' program that was listed at the beginning of this chapter. The **'for'** in the case of 'C' language constructs gets the variables initialised, there is a maximum or minimum limit & then an increment or decrement to the value of the variable. The moment the variable attains the value as indicated in the construct, the program stops execution. For e.g.

```
for (i=0;        i<24;        i++)

initialisation                increment
              Maximum value
```

In the case of an UNIX **'for'** loop the variable gets the values as words. Let us say you want to write a directory listing program. This is how your script will be

```
for i in * → Recall that * means all the files in the directory
do
  echo $i   ($i is the name of the file)
done
```

Explanation:

```
If we type
$ ls * <Ret>        (All the files get listed)
  birds
  games
  kb
  bk
  games1
$
```

One by one the variable "i" assumes the value of the file name and for every successful assumption of a file name {(i.e) "i" is not null } the next step is executed. If the script were saved in a file **'birds3'** and executed you would get the same output as if you have typed **'ls'.** Let us take another example. Type out the following script, creating a file **"num"**

```
for i in 1 2 3 4 5
do
  echo $i
done
```

Now run **num**

```
$ num <Ret>
  1
  2
  3
  4
  5
$
```

The variable **'i'** first assumes a value '1' then it displays '1' (echo $i). For the next round it assumes a value '2' and displays '2', (echo $i) and so on till **i** gets the value 5 and displays the same. Because there are no further values the **'for'** loop comes to an end and you are back to the $ prompt.

Observe that **'i'** does not have to be initialised for every pass made by the program. The old value automatically gets discarded for a new value.

We have seen that the variable in a **'for'** loop can get its value either expilicitly as in the second case or it can get it in the form of an output. There are other ways of passing values to the variable too. Let us see how.

* We will modify the second case to look like this

```
for i in $*
do
  echo $i
done
```

The difference is that you have to follow the command with the arguments as follows.

```
$ num 1 2 3 4 5  <Ret>
  1
  2
  3
  4
  5
$
```

Once again modify the file **"num"** as follows

```
echo "Enter the numbers"
read number
for i in $number
do
  echo $i
done
```

If you typed 100,200,4,7,9 against the prompt,' Enter the numbers , the output would be

```
$ number        <Ret>
  Enter the numbers
  100 200 4 7 9       <Ret>
  150
  200
  4
  7
  9
$
```

The numbers 100, 200, 4, 7, 9 will be assigned to the variable 'number'and for each non null value assumed by **'i'** from **'number',** the value of 'i' will be displayed

You are perhaps wondering about the need to create such scripts. After all we are not going to use an UNIX terminal to look at displays of 1, 2, 3, 4 & 5, whatever be the fanciful form they are displayed in. Right? So we should have a logical, meaningful application of the 'for' loop facility.

Suppose you want to rename a set of files
(remember, how we renamed one file earlier)
or
If you want to remove a set of files which are very old.
or
If you want to sort some file
or
You have a long list of recipes and you want to know which are the preparation that use Ginger, Brinjal & Onion.
or
You had a bunch of programs and you want to know which of these programs update/delete records of a certain set of files.

Applications are many. It is upto you to think of them.

Try out the following:

```
echo enter the word that you want to search for
read word
ls *.cob > check          { → Redirect ls output to a
                          {   file check
for i in check
do                        { →For every file in
                          { check search for the
                          { given string
grep $word $i  > ckl
echo $i
cat ckl
done
```

The above program will look for the word specified by you in all the **.cob** files in your directory

We will now take up a practical example. Sometimes we end up with responses like "command not found" or "file not found" against some command given by us. The Unix system actually goes through our PATH looking for the file that has been specified by us on the command line. Let us create a script that will simulate this search process. Create a file called **"pserch"**

```
echo " Your path is"
'$ PATH '
echo "enter the file that you want to locate"
read file
echo $ PATH > ek
sed s/:/ /g ek > do
for i in 'cat do'
  do
        find $i -name $file -print teen
        if grep $file teen
              then
                    echo File $file found in $i
              else
                    echo File $file not found in $i
        fi
  done
```

There is one command namely **"sed"** which we have not covered so far. This will be covered in the chapter on Special Utilities. **"sed"** is used here to replace the ":" in the PATH with spaces. Try out this program. This program is a more generalised version of the program **"fserch'** which can be used for a specific PATH only. Both the programs, the **"fserch** and **"pserch"** scan through the directories in your PATH and if you have any duplicate files in your PATH this will be brought out. You can then take necessary action.

We have so far used the **'for'** loop and the **'if'** statement. Let us look at the other two types of loops (i.e) the **'while'** loop & the **'until'** loop.

6.10

while loop

The **"while"** loop, as in the **"if"** statement is concerned only about the outcome of the command and not any particular value. We will look at the syntax first, before going on to a example

```
while {control command}
do
  command
done
```

Let us again look at the following syntax

```
  if control command
then
                commands
  fi
```

In the above construct as we have seen earlier, the commands immediately following 'then' get executed only if the 'if' is successful. In the **'while'** loop as long as the {while control command} returns a true value the loop will continue to be executed.

```
Let us examine the following
echo "enter the file name to be searched
read file
echo 'enter the word to search
read word
if grep $word $file  ckk
then
   echo "$word found in $file"
else
   echo "word not found in $file"
fi
```

In the above case the loop will get executed when the word is found and will echo "word not found' otherwise. In the case of **'cmp'** command we get a message only if the files are different. Similarly we should be able to write a script where by it continuously searches for a word in a set of files till the word is found as in the previous example. Only, we should use the **'while'** loop. But first we will learn of a new operator called **'shift'**.

6.11

shift

Recall the discussion on positional parameters $0, $1, $#, etc. Also recall the **'set'**command. With the 'set'command we could assign new values to $1, $2 etc., at any point in the script. Sometimes we may have an unknown number of arguments and we may not be able to hard code the program for a certain set of arguments. Say for example, you want to find the word 'getc' in all your files, you can't say in your script

```
$ grep getc file1 file2 file3 file...
```

because you do not know how many files you have nor do you know their names. Also you can't say

```
$ grep $1 $*
```

because $* represents all the arguments including the word that has to be searched. E.g., if the script is called **ser**

```
$ ser getc $*
```

because

$* will also include'getc', since getc is $1 and $* includes $1, $2, $3, $4 etc., So what is the answer?

Try **shift!!**

This is what **shift** does. Type

```
$ set 'date'
$ echo $1
  Mon
```

Now put the following in a file **"shi"**

```
set 'date'
echo $1
shift
echo $1
```

and run the program

```
$ shi
  mon
  Apr
$
```

What happened? Let us look at how the program worked

```
set 'date'
  mon   apr    27    07:10       ist    1962
   $1    $2    $3      $4        $5      $6
  echo  $1
  mon
  shift
  mon   apr    27    07:10 i     st     1962
        $1     $2    $3          $4     $5
  echo  $1
  apr
```

What happened to 'mon'? It is lost of course!

Let us make use of the 'shift'now with the **'while'** loop. Create a file as follows. Call it **s1.**

```
word=$1 →           Save the value of
shift               $1 in word
while grep $word $1
do
  shift
done
echo $word not found in $1 file
```

This program **s1** will continously scan the file or the files and will stop execution the moment it comes across a file that does not have the word specified. If you type

```
$ s1 boy *
  boy not found in shi file
$
```

Now **"shi"** may be the first file that has been searched or the "nth" file, but this is the first file where the search has been unsuccessful.

Let us look at a very straight forward **'while'** loop

```
number=1→   Initialise the value of number
while[ $number -le 5 ] → condition for while
do
  echo $number  → display the number
  number= 'expr $number +1' → increment number
done
```

The example above is a simple version of the **'while'** loop. Here the program is affected by an internal change rather than an external change like the list of files that came to an end. In this, the variable was first initialised to 1, then the loop was conditioned to execute as long as the value of number was less than 5. Then it exit the loop.

We will next go on to the **'until'** loop after touching upon the arithmetic operators used in UNIX.

6.12

arithmetic operators

The arithmetic comparison operators in the shell programming language are as follows:

-le	less than or equal to
-eq	Equal
-lt	less than
-ge	greater than or equal to
-gt	greater than
-ne	not equal to

You will be using these comparison operators in your shell programming.

Let us look at another example of **"while"** using the above operators. This example will also help in bringing out the difference between the **"while"** construct and the **"until"** construct. Enter the following in a file. Call the file **"wipe".**

```
n=0
  while [ $n -le 24]
  do
            echo "\n"
            n='expr $n + 1'
done
```

This program will clear the screen the way you wipe a blackboard.

6.13

until loop

The **'until'** loop can be considered to be an anti **'while'** loop. Look at the **'until'** loop syntax.

```
until {condition}
  do
            commands
done
```

This means that the commands within the **'do & done'** are to be executed as long as the condition is not true. But in the case of a **'while** loop' the command between **'do & done'** will be executed only if the condition is true. Do you know what your 'MAILCHECK' program does? It keeps checking your MAIL file periodically depending upon the time interval specified by you. Once it senses that there is a new entry in the MAILBOX, it informs the user that there is some new mail for him/her.

Let us try and create an imitation program with some assumptions.

We will assume that the program should check the mail file every 600 seconds or 10mts.,

```
# user name is mohan
# file name is mailfil
# to check files every 10mts.
  until [ test $mailfil = $chkfil ]
  do
            sleep 600
  done
  echo "mohan you have mail"
            cp $mailfil $chkfil
```

Please note that the above program is only to demonstrate a point. Unlike other scripts this script will not work in the present form.

Here as long as the **'mailfil'**is equal to **'chkfil** 'the program sleeps. It sleeps for 10mts(600 secs). If some new mail has come to the **'mailfil'** then its length will be greater than the **'chkfil'** which is nothing but a copy of **'mailfil'** before this mail arrived. So the 'loop' is broken and Mohan is intimated. Next the new **mailfil** is copied to **chkfil** and the program goes on.

Let us look at another example. This program will look for a word in a file or a group of files. The moment a file is found which contains the word specified, the program will stop execution.

Call the script **"locater'** and try it out yourself.

```
# This program will flag the first file
# where the word is found.
word =      $1 → Save the value of
shift       $1 in word
until grep $word $1
do
shift
done
echo $word found in $1 file
```

Let us rewrite the **wipe** program using the **"until"** construct. Create a file called **wipe1** as follows.

```
n=0
until [ $n = 24 ]
do
  echo "\n"
  n='expr $n + 1'
done
```

In the script **"wipe"**, blank lines were to be displayed as long as the value of variable 'n' was less than 24. In the case of script **"wipe1"** blank lines are to be displayed as long as the value of the variable 'n' was not equal to 24. The difference looks very subtle and it may be so but interchange the condition within the brackets for the **while** and **until** loops and see what happens. You may (unfortunately) have to resort to a trial and error approach before deciding between the **"while"** and **"until"** condition for a given problem. But then do not worry about making mistakes as long as it does not become a habit.

We have seen the **'if'** constructs (three types), the **'for'** loop, the **'while'** loop and the **'until'** loop. Before we go on to the other constructs let us look at a command called **'test'**.

You may have observed that we have been very generously using files either to **'grep'** or **'copy'** or **'rename'** taking their presence in the current working directory for granted. Suppose the file that you want to use is not present in the directory then what? Or if the file is present but is not readable then what do you do? All your shell programming will come to naught if these simple things are not checked for. You could perhaps write a script that will check the various permission bits or the very availability of the file. Each new program that you write should incorporate this script This will be quiet painful. To relieve you of this misery, UNIX has provided us with the **'test'** command.

6.14

'test' command The **'test'** command works in conjunction with the **'if'** command for

**** Numerical comparisons
**** String comparisons
**** File permissions
**** Success/failure of commands

Recall the 'if' constructs.

```
if grep $word Mon.cob >> /usr/temp
then
   echo $word found
fi
```

This can be written as

```
if test grep $word mon.cob >>  /usr/temp
then
   echo "$word found"
fi
```

There is one other thing that needs to be mentioned here. That is the 'status' of a command. A command may be successful or it may not be successful. If we give a command such as

```
$ cp file1 file2
$ echo $?  → This command is successful
  0
$
```

Next

```
$ cp filex file1
  file not found  → This command is not successful
$ echo $?
  1
$
```

What is meant by the output of **"$"?** Here if the answer is 0 it means the command is successful; If it is non zero then the command is a failure. This is called the **'exit'** status of a command or a program. Normally we may not need to know the exit status of a single command typed on the command line. But, if within a shell script one command depends upon the success or failure of another command then it becomes very critical.

In the case of a statement like

```
if grep $ word mon.cob > /usr/temp
```

the 'if' is not concerned with the output of the **'grep'** but only if it **(grep)** is a success or failure.

The **'test'** command when used, returns '0' if the command is successful and '1' if it fails. The "$?" displays the exit status of the preceding command.

6.14.1

String comparison: The following operators are used by **"test"**.

```
=  Equal
!= Not equal
-z Zero length string
-n Non zero length
```

If an user were to type

```
$ cp money <Ret>
```

the system would display an error message & indicate the correct syntax. Let us write a similar script.

```
r=$#
if test r -lt 2 -o -s$1 -o -s$2
then
  echo command incomplete
  echo usage cp file1 file2
else
            cp $1 $2
  echo $1 copied to $2
fi
```

6.14.2

Numeric values: We have already seen the numeric operations. The **'test'** uses numeric operators as above. But don't get mixed by string equality & numeric equality.

100 = 100 → As string they are equal
100 -eq 100.00 → Numerically they are equal
100 = 100.00 → Not correct

At the outset of the introduction to **test,** we spoke about the read permission of files or write permission of files. The **'test'** command uses the following.

Attribute	Meaning
-r file	Readable file
-w file	Writable file
-d file	Directory file
-s file	Non zero file
-p file	Fifo file
-f file	Ordinary file

Supposing you intend to copy a file, then you should first check if the file exists and if it is readable. Here's how

```
if test -r $1
then
   cp $1 $2
else
   echo 'can't copy this file/not readable
fi
```

Of course we assume that you have checked if all the arguments are correct.

Unstructured looping remains to be seen as far as shell programming is concerned. Before we go onto this construct, let us examine the following topics.

6.15

.profile

variables (i.e) user defined and shell variables. We also touched briefly on how using these shell variables we could tailor an environment suitable to the user. This was done by changing the user's HOME DIRECTORY or the Primary prompt etc. If the changes that we make have to be permanent then we must put them in the **'.profile'** file of user's HOME DIRECTORY. The **.profile** is in the HOME directory because the moment you login, the system connects you to the HOME directory and looks for the **.profile** file to execute. The name **.profile** itself is very suggestive.

We have so far written several scripts to find a word, to copy a file, to rename a file etc. If you put all these files in a directory called **'myacts'** you can then include it in your

PATH so that these commands can be executed from anywhere within the directories in which you are authorised to work.

```
$ cat profile                <Ret>
HOME =/usr/train/mohan              → Your original profile file
MAIL =/usr/train/mail/mohan
PATH =.:/bin/usr/oracle:/usr/unix
TERM =VT100
export HOME MAIL PATH TERM
```

You can modify the profile file to look like

```
HOME =/usr/train/mohan
MAIL =/urs/train/mail/mohan
PATH=$HOME/myacts:/bin:/usr/oracle:/usr/unix
TERM=VT100
PS1="MOHAN"
PS2="NEW"
export HOME MAIL PATH TERM PS1 PS1
echo Welcome to the unix session
echo KLASS COMPUTERS
banner Welcome
echo The users already logged in are
who
echo you may begin your unix session
echo logout when you end your session
```

Note:

(1) PATH has been modified to include the directory **'myacts'.** Instead of (.) $HOME has been used.

(2) The prompt will now be 'MOHAN ' and not '$'

(3) It will display a message 'Welcome to unix '. Next it will display 'Welcome' in banner format.

(4) It will display all those who are logged in

(5) Finally it will ask you to logout when you end your session.

Along the same lines you can add to or modify the .profile to suit the needs of the user.

6.16

special character So far we have seen some special characters like >, \etc. Given below are most of the special characters and shell variables.

CHARACTER	MEANING / FUNCTION
$#	Total number of positional parameters
$0	Command name
$*	All the parameters
$n	nth positional parameter
\	Continue command on next line
file	Use file as output file
	Use file as input file
>file	Append to end of file
*,?,[]	Wildcard substitution
&	Run the job as background process
$?	Exit status of preceding command
2{filename}	Send error message to file
$$	Display PID of present shell
'x'&&'y'	Execute 'y' if 'x' is successful
'x'//'y'	Execute 'y' if 'x' is a failure
#	Comment line
' '	Interpret enclosed characters literally
" "	Interpret enclosed character literally except for $ combination and * which will be expanded.

6.17

Redirection: A note on redirection is a must here. So far we have been using the ">" to redirect the output to a file or the "<" to take input from a file. But what about the error messages ? Usually the error messages are displayed on the screen thus.

```
$ mv hames sport
  mv: cannot open hames
$
```

However, if you have submitted a command such that it is executed as a background process it becomes a different matter altogether. If due to some error the program comes to a halt you will not know the reason unless you execute it as an ordinary process and look at the error message. The easier method is to direct all the error messages to a file and look at the file later for any action if necessary. This is how it is done:

```
$ mv hames sport 2 >erfill
$
$ cat erfill
  mv: cannot open hames
$
```

Now what is meant by "2" in the above example? The standard input as you know is the keyboard, the standard output is the terminal. The standard error is also the terminal. This is why the error messages get displayed on the terminal. Within the Unix system, these three are referred as follows:

0 : Standard Input
1 : Standard Output
2 : Standard Error

0,1 and 2 are actually "file descriptors" or rather pointers to the files. So by specifying "2" the standard error gets directed to the files specified.

Now back to looping.

6.18

the case statement

The UNIX 'case' statement offers a multi-way branching depending upon the user input or a value assigned to a variable from within the program. Let us look at an example of a menu that is often seen in application programs to-day.

MAIN MENU

1. MASTER MAINTENANCE
2. QUERY CUSTOMER BALANCE
3. REPORTS MODULE
4. EXIT

ENTER YOUR CHOICE [1 TO 4]

The program would look something like this.

```
echo " MAIN MENU "
echo " 1. MASTER MAINTENANCE "
echo " 2. QUERY CUSTOMER BALANCE "
echo " 3. REPORTS MODULE "
echo " 4. EXIT "
echo " ENTER YOUR CHOICE [ 1 TO 4 ] : "
read choice
case $ choice in
1) echo "This is the master maintenance module" ;;
2) echo "This is the enquiry module" ;;
3) echo "This is the reports module" ;;
4) exit ;;
*) echo "wrong choice, try again";;
esac
```

In this case the shell compares the value in the variable **choice** with the option given i.e. 1,2,3 or 4. If '1' is entered then 'master maintenance' is executed, if '2' is entered by the user the 'query' program is executed and so forth. If something other than 1,2,3 or 4 is entered the wrong choice message is echoed. The standard syntax is

```
case $ option in
pattern -1)
   commands -1
   commands -1 ;;
pattern -2)
   commands -2 ;;


esac
```

The value in **'option'** is matched with each 'pattern' till a match is found or the 'esac' statement is encountered. The 'case' construct is straight forward and very powerful. The variable for comparison can get its value from the user or from within the program.

The program which we looked at just now will work. But due to obvious limitations the program will bring you back to the system prompt every time. Let us modify the program a little bit and see. Now make the following changes.

```
choice=0
while [ $choice = 0]
do
tput clear
echo "                    MAIN MENU "
echo "\n\n"
echo "1. MASTER MAINTENANCE "
echo "\n\n"
echo "2. QUERY CUSTOMER BALANCE "
echo "\n\n"
echo "3. REPORTS MODULE "
echo "\n\n"
echo "4. EXIT "
echo "\n\n\n"
echo "ENTER YOUR CHOICE [1 TO 4] : \c "
read choice
Case $ Choice in
1) echo "This is the master maintenance module "
sleep 2;;
2) echo "This is the enquiry module " sleep 2 ;;
3) echo "This is the reports module " sleep 2;;
4) echo "exiting the program.....!!"
exit;;
*) echo "wrong choice !!!!! TRY AGAIN"
continue;;
esac
done
```

This program will do the same job as the previous version. But this version is a better version to work with. Also you will not be brought to the system prompt every time you choose an option.

If you have taken up the job of copying files to appropriate directories and the type of files are **.cob** files, **.exe** file and **.dbf** files, then the possible script could be

```
for file in *
do
case $file in
*.cob )
```

```
cp $file /usr/COBOL;;
*.exe )
  cp $file /usr/games;;
*.dbf )
  cp $file /usr/prg;;
*.* )
  cp $file /usr/misc;;
esac
done
```

The above program reads a set of files & for every file received, it passes the file name as a value to the 'case' statement. The case statement evaluates the name for a pattern (i.e.) ***.cob** or ***.exe** or ***.dbf.** If the file name matches any of these patterns then the corresponding action is taken. If the file does not match any of the three patterns the file is copied to the **/misc** directory.

This example was to demonstrate that the case construct can be assigned values from within or without the program.

6.19

'case' Vs 'if'

On seeing the 'case' construct you may perhaps think why use 'case' when one can very easily use 'if'. After all the following 'case' construct can be rewritten as.

```
case $ option in        if test $ option = '1'
1) command 1;;          then
2) command 2;;          command 1
*) command 3;;          elif test $ option = '2'
  esac                  then
  else
  command 3
  fi
```

This line of thinking is not incorrect. But in the 'case' construct shown above the code is very compact. Further the 'test'command is an UNIX command and to execute it a new subshell has to be created every time it is used by the program. And this naturally takes time. Therefore in situations like this it is recommended that the case statement be used.

Well three cheers for the "case" statement.

6.20

shell functions

Now as a programmer who wants to build and improve on the work done by others it is not enough if you merely write some interesting shell scripts. You must go atleast one step further. Remember, you are supposed to create an user-friendly environment for your fellow users. One usual complaint about the Unix system is that you always have to use the **'pwd'**command to get your bearings. In the case of MSDOS this does not happen. Usually in the "autoexec.bat" file a simple command [prompt pg] is inserted which will ensure that the present working directory is always displayed as the prompt. When such an user migrates from MS DOS to the UNIX environment he is definitely not going to like to have to use **'pwd'** every time. Now the actual commands to display the working directory as the user moves around are very simple. They are

```
cd $1
PS1 = 'pwd'
```

But if these commands are executed as a shell script they will not do the trick. The answer to this is very simple. Write a shell function!!. There are two ways you can use the shell function. 1. Write a shell function as follows

```
$ chdir ()
  NEW {
  NEW cd $1
  NEW PS1 = 'pwd'
  NEW }
$
```

OBSERVATION

1. The simple brackets "()" tells the shell that this is a function or a script. The shell will then display the secondary prompt.
2. "NEW" is the secondary prompt.
3. "{" means the commencement of the body of the function.
4. "}" means the end of the function. You will now be returned to the primary prompt.

Now if you type

```
$ chdir /usr/train/ram        <Ret>
/usr/train/ram
```

the prompt displayed will be the present working directory. Whenever you have to change directories make use of the **"chdir"** function. But this method has one drawback. The moment you logout the function will also disappear. So when you login again you will have to rewrite the function. This is not very user- friendly is it ?. The second method is a more practical one. Let us see.

2. Simply define the above function **"chdir"** in your **.profile** file.

The function will reside in the memory every time you login. Since the function is part of the **.profile** it will also get executed. But do not overdo the function bit because the functions defined thus will reside in the memory and will end up in slowing up your system. So use your discretion when you create functions.

debugging

Before we wind up this chapter on shell programming. Let us look at methods that will help us debug our shell scripts. Earlier in this chapter we had seen how the **'test'** statement can check the file status. Also with the use of $* & $# we could ensure that the user entered the right number of arguments.

But if a program were to terminate because of an error in the middle and if the program is like a typical UNIX program (non-communicative) then we will not know where the error has occured. If we type

```
$ $?          exit status
1             probable response
$
```

This does not tell us much, does it?

Remember that an exit status of '0' means the program is successful. Any non-zero exit status will mean error. Since this is the case why not introduce our own exit status. Let us look at a simple copy program.

```
$ cat  > copy
#version 1 of 'copy' program
  echo "Enter source file"
  read f1:
  echo "Enter destination file"
  read f2
  cp $f1 $2
  echo "$f1 copied to $f2
```

If this program were to be written such that the command-line were used, the script would be just

```
copy $1 $2
```

Can you think of the potential errors ? Let's create a script that will handle the errors.

```
# Version 2 of 'copy' program
  if [ $# -le 1 ]
  then
            echo "Argument list is incomplete"
            echo usage is copy file1 file2
            exit 1
  elif [ $# -gt 2 ]
            echo "Argument list too long"
            echo usage is copy file1 file2
            exit 2
  elif test ! -f $1
            then
            echo $1 not found
            exit 3
  elif test ! -r $1
            then
            echo "file is not readable"
            exit 4
  elif test ! -w $2
            then
            echo file $2 exists, not writable
            exit 5
else
            cp $1 $2
            echo: The file $1 has been copied to $2
fi
```

A rather long script, compared to version 1, but this takes care of errors that come from incomplete typing and errors that arise out of giving wrong names. Notice that at every **'if'** the **'exit'** statement has been used. By getting the display of an exit status we can know where the error has occurred. Here of course the echo statement tells us all. But if the **'copy'** program were part of another program, then the exit status of this **'copy'** program can be used by the main program to do what has to be done in a given event. Well this is one method of finding out where exactly your program ran into trouble. Many programmers are in the practice of introducing **"echo"** statements at various levels in the program so that by means of these statements or flags they can trace the execution of their program. Unix itself has options to the shell **"sh"** command (surprised?!). We will discuss these options now and see how they help the programmer to take a look at the progress or otherwise of his pet script.

First the **"v"** option. Let us take a simple program that we have created namely **"seal"**. This program will rename a given file as "filename.username". Now type

```
$ cat seal  <Ret>
  # this program renames a file(s)
  file=$1
  shift
  set 'who am i'
  for i in file
            do
            mv $file $file.$1
  done
$
```

Now execute the program using the **"-v"** option. Type

```
$ sh -v seal games  <Ret>
  # This program renames a file(s)
  file=$1
  shift
  set 'who am i'
            do
                 mv $file $file.$1
$
```

The **"-v"** option printed all the lines that were executed. If at any line there was an error of syntax it would have flagged the same. Let us go on to the next option that is the **"-x"** option.

```
$ sh -x seal games1          <Ret>
file=games1
  +shift
  +who am i
  +set mohan tty01 Nov 10 17:17
  +mv games1 games1 .mohan
$
```

This option displays the result of every line that gets executed. You can see how the variable **"file"** gets assigned the value of **"games1"**. Then you saw the result of the **"who am i"** command as it was executed. Finally you saw the substitution that took place in the line **"mv $file $file.$1"**

Now let us go for the mixed fruit jam! We will use the **"-v"** and the **"-x"** options together and see what happens. Type:

```
$ sh -vx seal kb          <Ret>
  # This program renames a file(s)
  file=$1
  file=kb
  shift
   +shift
  set 'who am i'
   +who am i
   +set mohan tty01 Nov 10 17:17
  mv $file $file.$1
   +mv kb kb.mohan
$
```

There is much more about debugging. You can use the SYMBOLIC DEBUGGER **"sdb"** or the **"adb"** for debugging your programs. We will not go into those facilities at this stage.

Conclusion

As a conclusion let us review the features of the shell (the bourne shell)

- → It is interactive
- → It allows looping
- → It allows command execution
- → It can take arguments from the command line
- → It allows file creation
- → Allows execution of commands on a condition
- → Variable can be defined and used
- → Variable can be used in a restricted place or throughout the program
- → Allows you to write generalised scripts
- → Allows use of wild card characters
- → Use of subroutines
- → Use of shell function

In order to create the various scripts we were aided by various constructs. The various constructs we have seen are the **"for"** loop, the **"if"** construct with **'else'** & **'elif'**. Next we worked on two other loops namely the **"until"** and the **"while"** loops. Finally we saw the **"case"** constructs.

During the course of this chapter new commands introduced were **"set"**, **"read"**, **'test"**, **"shift"**. Well that is quite an arsenal! Now that you are well armed you can tackle many of the routine situations that arise in your day to day activity. Happy Hunting!!

EXERCISE

1. Having created a shell script with the name "greet", can you execute it by simply typing : [$ greet]?
2. How can we export a variable to its parent shell?
3. Write a shell script to copy one file to another. The script should prompt the user to enter the source and destination files. Also display a suitable message after the job is completed.
4. Write a shell script to rename a file. Do not use the "mv" command in the shell script.
5. Write a script that lets you convert a file into an executable file.
6. Write a script to copy one file to another using command line arguments.

7. set date. What is $1 and $6.

8. Given a file name the script should echo a suitable message depending upon the file type

9. Write a script to perform the above. The program should terminate if the file name is given as "ADIOS'.

10. Your script should read another script and inform the user on the nature of construct used.

11. Write a script to display the following:
    1 2 3 4 5

12. Try out the following script.
    ```
    for i in 'cal'
    do
    echo $i
    done
    ```
    Count the number of lines in output.

13. In how many ways can the variable in a "for" script get/be assigned values? What are they?

14. Write a program to locate a word in a group of files. The program must stop execution when it encounters the given word for the third time.

15. Write a script that will perform the necessary operation on the two numbers entered by the user, depending upon the operator entered. The program should be menu-driven.

16. Create a shell script using the "case" construct such that it performs all the checks of the "copy" program Version 2.

7

SPECIAL UTILITIES

So far we have been leading you along rather slowly. And rightly so. At the beginning of the book you were a novice but now you have learnt the various commands available in the UNIX repertoire. You have also gone through the shell programming concepts. (You have completed all the exercises given so far? !!) So now you know quiet a lot, right? On this confident note let us do some work using the "Special Utilities".

UNIX, as you know is a collection of programs. When UNIX was first released it had just enough programs to execute the basic functions of an Operating System. This can be thought of as Vanilla UNIX. (Computers & Icecreams ! What a combination!) Later, various users of UNIX added their own functions to the UNIX Operating System. One such utility is **'awk'.** This chapter is devoted to utilities like **awk, sed, grep.** You will realise that you can work wonders with the UNIX operating System and the special utilities.

7.1 grep

We have discussed **'grep'** earlier in Getting Started with UNIX and Shell Programming chapters. Here we will take a more detailed look at grep. **'grep'** is the acronym for "globally search for regular expressions and print them". **'grep'** is an excellent feature which allows you to locate a given pattern in a file or files without having to open the file(s) using an editor.

'grep' also has cousins by the name **'fgrep'** & **'egrep'.** We will get acquainted with them too.

Our previous reference to **'grep'** was limited. We covered the following.

1) grep 'word'fileto locate a word.

2) grep 'string' fileto locate a string

3) grep word/string to locate a string or word in all files in a directory

4) who : grep Mohan grep in conjunction with other commands

Let us now look at other features of grep.

7.1.1 Regular expression

Suppose in your document you are refering to your friend Amar, and you would like to know the lines which have Amar. So you type

```
$ grep Amar doc  <Ret>
```

[All lines containing 'Amar'are displayed.]

But what if you have written Amar as 'amar'? Here you use the 'regular expression' idea.

```
$ grep[ '[Aa]mar' doc  <Ret>
```

[All lines containing 'Amar' and 'amar' are displayed.]

From a file of employee records you could select all employees with names starting from A to M by giving the following command.

```
$ grep [ A-M ].* emp  <Ret>
```

[All records with names like Amar, Bala, Ivan, Lakshmi, Mohan etc., will get listed.]

NOTE:

Here "*" is used to signify any number of characters because the name could be Amar or Amirthalingam.

7.1.2 -L option

If you wanted to know only the file names of the files containing the word then type

```
$ grep -l "word" *     <Ret>
```

7.1.3

-v option

If you want to take a listing of all lines that don't match a pattern. For e.g., if you have a file called **'emp',** which contain fields as follows.

01 Ramesh	Finance	Finance Manager	6000
02 Ganesh	Accounts	Accounts Manager	6000
03 Ganapathy	Finance	Junior Officer	4000
04 Mohan	Finance	Section Sup'dent	4000
05 Ramani	Accounts	Section Sup'dent	3500
06 Zakir	Marketing	Sales Executive	3975

If you want to list out all the staff who do not belong to finance department, type

```
$ grep -v "Finance" emp <Ret>
  02 Ganesh   Accounts    Accounts Manager 6000
  05 Ramani   Accounts    Section Sup'dent  3500
  06 Zakir    Marketing   Sales Executive   3975
$
```

The **'-v'** option reverses the effect (i.e) all lines that do not match the given pattern get displayed.

7.1.4

'^' option

If you want to take a listing of a 'C' program without the comment lines then you have to print all lines that do not begin with the # symbol. So type

```
$ grep -v "^ #" prog.c  <Ret>
```

The "^" does the trick. It helps you list all the lines which do not begin with the pattern. In this case all line that do not begin will the # are listed. To count the total number of lines, the **-c** option is used.

7.1.5

-c option

```
$ grep -c "pattern" doc        <Ret>
  n  (where 'n' is an integer)
$
```

If you want to know all people drawing a salary of Rs.6000, type

```
$ grep "6000"emp      <Ret>
  01 Ramesh  Finance       Finance Manager  6000
  02 Ganesh  Accounts      Accounts Manager 6000
$
```

7.1.6

"$" option

If you want the records of employees whose salary ends with '5' then

```
$ grep '5$' emp        <Ret>
  06 Zakir     Marketing Sales Executive      3975
$
```

Now let us look at cousins **'fgrep & egrep'. fgrep** means fast grep and egrep means extended grep.

7.2

fgrep

fgrep as said above is faster than **grep** & **egrep.** It accomodates more than one pattern but cannot discern regular expressions. **fgrep** can accept the pattern(s) to be matched from a file or from the command line.

In the chapter on Shell Programming we spoke of locating recipes which use potato, brinjal & onion, right? Now create a file

```
$ cat >veg        <Ret>
  potato
  brinjal
  onion ( ^d )
$
```

Next type

```
$ fgrep -f veg recl    <Ret>
```

[The **-f** option before **'veg'** indicates that **"veg"** is a file and the contents of the file should be used as patterns for search from the file recl]

However if you were to type

```
$ fgrep [Aa]mar doc       <Ret>
$
```

the **'fgrep'** does not display any lines because it does not understand regular expressions. But it searches for a pattern exactly like '[Aa]mar' and hence comes back empty handed.

7.3

egrep

Cousin **'egrep'**is faster than **'grep'** but slower than **'fgrep'.** It makes up for this shortcoming by being able to perform extended functions hence the name - 'extended grep'. Let us see what they are.

7.3.1

regular expression If you were to put the value [Aa]mar in a file 'g' and type

```
$ egrep -f g doc          <Ret>
```

All lines containing the word 'Amar' or 'amar' will get displayed

7.3.2

multiple regular Expression

egrep can also accept 'multiple regular expressions'. Suppose from the file **'emp'** you want to print all people whose name starts with 'R' and whose designation is Manager, type

```
$ cat >mux          <Ret>
  R.* Manager
$
```

Now type

```
$ egrep -f mux emp                  <Ret>
  01 Ramesh  Finance      Finance Manager   6000
$
```

In situations where you have two parts for a name (i.e.) Ramesh Krishnaswamy or Ganesh Subramanian, here also you can use multiple expressions. E.g.,

```
R.* K.*
```

(This means a line containing a word starting with R plus zero or more characters, a space and a word starting with K followed by zero or more characters)

7.3.3

the 'or'option

The 'or' option is denoted by | (pipe). You can ask **'egrep'** to print lines which meet the first pattern or the second pattern.

```
$ egrep Manager : Finance emp <Ret>
  01 Ramesh  Finance    Finance Manager   6000
  02 Ganesh  Accounts   Accounts Manager 6000
$
```

We will sum up the **grep, fgrep** & **egrep** commands as follows.

Command	**Action**
grep (pattern) file name	Will search for pattern in a file
{ pattern } file1 file2	Will search for pattern in multiple files
-l { pattern } *	Will list all files which contain pattern
-n { pattern } file	Will list lines with line number
.[Aa] * file	All lines containing words starting with A or a
-v { pattern } file	All lines that do not contain pattern
-c { pattern } file	Count no. of lines containing the pattern
" ^ x" file	All lines beginning with 'x'
' x $ ' file	All lines ending with 'x'
fgrep -f sf file	Will read patterns from file 'sf'
egrep -f sf file	Will read patterns from file 'sf'
egrep x.* y.* file	Will display all lines containing words starting with x and the next word starting with y
egrep A* | B* file	Display lines with either words starting with A or words starting with B

7.4

sed

We have so far confined our activities to locating the occurance of a word(s) in a file. But what if you wanted to locate the word and introduce/substitute another word. Again, what if you wanted to delete all lines in the file which fall before/after the first occurance of a given pattern. To meet these requirements you need the services of a stream editor i.e. **'sed'.**

In order to work on some live data create the following files.

(1) games

Football, played by twenty two, all active, Germany, world cup
Hockey, played by twenty two, all active England, world cup
Cricket, played by twenty two, some active, Australia, B & H series
Squash, singles and doubles, all active Pakistan, all England cup
Tennis, singles and doubles, all active U.S. Wimbledon
Boxing, individual, all active U.S. W.B.F.

(2) sundry

Bulbs	Electrical	5.10	4
Pen	Stationery	3.50	2
Pads	Stationery	4.00	5
LCD	Electronic	4.00	1
Potentiometer	Electronic	5.00	2
Paper clips	Stationery	4.00	100
Pencil	Stationery	0.50	1
Gloves	Personal	9.00	2
Key chain	Personal	3.00	1

Having created the files let us get to work using **'sed'.** The basic syntax of **'sed'** and the rules are as follows.

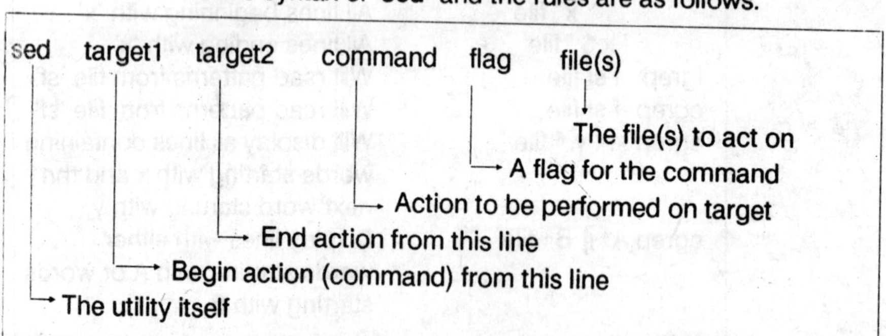

A rather long winded syntax, is it not? But wait, don't panic! There is some good news. You don't have to specify every thing for every action you want to perform on the target file(s). For example take the case of substitution

7.4.1

substitution

```
$ sed 's Electrical/Household/q'  sundry
                                    └──→ file name
                              └→ global (i.e for every line)
                   └→ New word
          └──→ Word to be replaced
    └→ s(substitute)
└→ Utility
```

OBSERVATION:

* The command is enclosed in 'single quotes' so that special characters are not interpretted by the shell.
* The 'g' is a flag that means perform the command (substitution) globally
* /electrical/ The word to be replaced. MUST BE GIVEN WITHIN SLASHES ONLY
* Household/ The replacement word
* Since no target lines are given, this command examines every line and replaces the word 'electrical' with 'household' wherever the word electrical is present
* An important point to note is that the **'sed'** leaves the original file unchanged. So if you want the modified file also to be stored or printed, then you have to specifically say so. How this is done, we will see shortly.

7.4..1a

substitution by reference

We have seen global substitution. But suppose you want to replace a word which occurs in a particular line which has another word, "word1" then what would you do? Here the second word (i.e) "word1" is the reference.

So this is what you do

```
$ sed '/Pads/ s/Stationery/printing/' sundry    <Ret>
  Pads printing 4.00 5
$
```

Here the **'sed'** searched the file for the line containing the word 'Pads'. Having got that line it looked for the word 'Stationery' and replaced it with the word 'printing'.

In this case giving the flag **'g'** will not make any difference. But if you have more than one line with the words 'Pads' & 'Stationery', then specifying **'g'** will make the changes in all the lines.

In the previous example we used one parameter or context namely 'Pads', **'sed'** was instructed to substitute 'Stationery' with 'printing'.Let us become more specific. If you want to change a word in a line which contains the word 'twenty' but from a particular line then this is what you do.

```
$ sed '2,/twenty/ s/all/every body/' games <Ret>
```

(Note that the flag **'g'** has not been used here)

Here we have used the line number '2' to indicate that **'sed'** should implement the command from line '2'. Here only the first occurance of "all" after line number two is substituted.

We can also specify a range of lines on which the command should act. E.g.,

```
$ sed '2,6 s/all/every body/' games <Ret>
```

Enough of substitution. Let us delete some lines from the file. Let us delete the fourth line.

7.4.2

deletion

```
$ sed '4 d' games        <Ret>
```

If you want a range of lines deleted then type

```
$ sed '3,5 d' sundry        <Ret>
```

7.4.3

write option

All along you were getting the modified data displayed on the screen, while the original file remained intact. Very convenient, because you may issue a command to delete some lines by chance and this could cause a lot of grief. However, if you wanted the modified data to be stored permanently, then what! **'sed'** very thoughtfully provides us with a flag that will write the modified contents to another file.

```
$ sed '2,/twenty/all/every body/w games5' games
$
```

the new file **'games5'** does not exist, it will be created. If it exists it will be overwritten. Make sure that the file name you give is a new one or the name of a file you do not need anymore and is *'writeable'* by you.

So now we move to the big boys league. You can tie your shoe laces yourself now, right?

7.4.4

the "-f" option Having looked at single command execution through **'sed'**, we will now go on to multiple command execution with **'sed'**. How does **'sed'** do it ?

In the case of **'grep'** the target file was searched for the first word and then a second pass was made for the second word/expression, which we wanted to locate. Let us see how **'sed'** performs this cycle.

Create a file called **'stest'**

```
s/all/everyman/g
q
```

Now type

```
$ sed -f stest games          <Ret>
  Football, played by twenty two, every man active,
  Germany, World cup
$
```

What happened? Our first command was to substitute the word 'all' with 'every man'. And to do the substitutions for all lines. But only one line was acted upon. Why? Because the next line says **'q'** which means 'quit'. So on every line of the target file every command in the command file is performed. No wonder, **'sed'** means stream editor. It reads the target file line by line and performs all action before reading the next line from the target file.

7.4.5

the "-e" option If only two or three changes have to be made to a file you do not really need to create a file. You can give the commands directly on the command line e.g.,

```
$ sed -e 's/Stationery/printing/' -e 's/Electronic/
   quartz/' sundry              <Ret>
```

We have made use of the **'-e'** option. The -e has to be placed before each instruction to inform **'sed'** that this command line contains more than one command.

7.4.6

the "i\" option Let us now add text to a file. Our files (i.e.,) **games** and **sundry** have no heading. Let us give it a heading. Create a file **'heading'** as follows.

```
$ Cat > heading         <Ret>
1i\
```

This is a sample file to test the commands under the stream editor.

Now run the **'sed'** command as

```
$ sed -f heading games  <Ret>
  If this file has to be stored you can redirect it.
$ sed -f heading games >>hgames
$
```

7.4.7

the "a\" option You can similarly add text after a line. Instead of **'i'** you have to use **'a'**. (Remember vi - 'i' to insert before and 'a' to append after)

Create a file **"tailor"**

```
$ Cat > tailor              <Ret>
6a\
The above is a list of details of popular games played.
```

Run the file and see what happens.

7.4.8

the "p" option Now let us take a look at printing with **'sed'**

```
$ sed 's/electrical/mechanical/p' sundry <Ret>
```

This prints the modified file on the printer. Following are the steps. It is necessary to go through these steps so that we can understand the next option better.

1 The target file is copied line by line to a buffer.

2 If the first line matches a given reference or if no reference/context is given, then the command is implemented (in this case substitution) on all the lines. If the command is successful then this buffer is printed and then emptied. [THE PRINTING AND FLUSHING OF THE BUFFER IS DONE SUBJECT TO THE SUCCESS OF THE COMMAND] (MODIFIED LINE IS PRINTED)

3 The buffer is printed if the command is not implemented. [ORIGINAL LINE IS PRINTED]

If we want only the modified lines then we must supress the third step above. This is done with the help of the **-n** option.

```
$ sed -n 's/electrical/mechanical/p' sundry <Ret>
```

Only those lines that are modified get printed.

7.4.9

!p option

If you want to create a file that does not match a pattern use the **!p** option.

```
$ sed -n '/electronic/ !p' sundry      <Ret>
```

All lines not having the pattern 'electronic' will be printed.

What we have seen so far is by no means the full story of **'sed'**. A good workout with the feature covered so far will make you a very good **'sed'** user. Combination of flags, using **'!'** to negate the command etc can give you all sorts of output. How well you use **'sed'** will depend upon your application

7.5

awk

The command **'grep'** lets you locate words or patterns in a file. Next **'sed'** lets you add or delete lines depending upon a pattern. You could replace the words or change the case and so forth. Now we come to the granddaddy of utilities i.e. **'awk'**. **'awk'** stands for Aho, Weinberger & Kernighan, the creators of this utility.

'awk' can do pattern matching, print selected records/fields and comparison & computation. That is quiet a lot !

We will take a look at how **'awk'** operates. **'awk'** operates like **'sed'** i.e. it processes the input line by line. Also it has to have a 'context' or 'reference'. The similarity ends here. When it comes to actions to be performed on the selected lines **'awk'** provides you a lot more features. We will use the **'sundry'** file once again.

A typical awk statement looks like this.

```
awk awk-command file name
```

```
awk '/stationery/ {print $1, $4}' sundry
```

OBSERVATIONS

1. The **'awk's** command portion is enclosed in single quotes
2. Within the single quotes the action portion is enclosed in curly braces.
3. There is a line specifier or a pattern to be matched which is enclosed in slashes.

What is the output? As an output against the above command. The first & fourth field of every record (line) of the file is printed. Provided ofcourse the record has a word **'stationery'**.

Let us understand the concept of fields, records and database files. Take a look at the **'sundry'** file again.

```
Cat sundry                              <Ret>
Bulbs             Electrical    5.10      4
Pen               Stationery    3.50      2
Pads              Stationery    4.00      5
LCD               Electronic    4.00      1
Potentiometer     Electronic    5.00      2
Paper clips       Stationery    4.00    100
Pencil            Stationery    0.50      1
Gloves            Personal      9.00      2
Key chain         Personal      3.00      1
```

There are 9 items listed. The entry for each item is called a 'record'. The **sundry** file therefore has NINE records. Now each record for example (Pen) has particulars that describe it, like name (Pen), type (Stationery), rate (3.50) and qty (2). Each of these particulars is a field. Hence a record in the **'sundry'** file has four fields. A file can have more than nine records and four fields. In database jargon record is considered as a row and the fields are considered as columns. So the **'sundry'** file has Nine rows and four columns. Now you will not confuse with records or rows with fields, right ! Now there has to be a separator between two fields. In **'awk'** a space or a tab is the default field separator. And the record separator is the 'NEW LINE' character, which is given by pressing the 'RETURN' or 'ENTER' KEY. Back to **'awk'!** We have seen a typical **'awk'** syntax. **'awk'** takes the input record by record (substituted for line by line) from the database table/file (substituted for file).

7.5.1

awk's 'rules of the thumb'.

1. *If no pattern is specified, it prints all records.*
2. *If no action is specified, all fields get printed.*

```
$ awk '{print} sundry <Ret>
```

prints all lines

```
$ awk '/personal/' sundry  <Ret>
```

prints entire records that has a field 'personal'

3. *If '{print $0}' is given in the command all fields are printed.*

7.5.2

Column selection You can select a specific column or a specific field of every record.

```
$ awk '{print $1}'sundry          <Ret>
```

will display the first field of every record. Which is the same as the first column of the file.

NOTE

$1 represents the first field, $2 represents the second field and so forth. $0 represents all the fields.

7.5.3 regular expression:

The use of regular expression in **'awk'** is the same as in **'sed'** & **'grep'**. e.g.

```
$ awk '/[A-M] .*{print $0 }'sundry        <Ret>
```

All fields of records which have a pattern whose first character is any alphabet between A and M (A & M also included) will be displayed.

'awk' can also ignore case if specified

7.5.4 numerical operations

```
$ awk '$4 >  3' sundry          <Ret>
Bulbs         Electrical     5.10   4
Pads          Stationery     4.00   5
Paper clips   Stationery     4.00   100
$
```

[All records where $4 (qty) is greater than 3 will be displayed.]

```
$ awk '$3 = =4' sundry                <Ret>
  Pads          Stationery    4.00   5
  LCD           Electronic    4.00   1
  Paper clips   Stationery    4.00   100
$
```

NOTE :
'= =' is the equal to operator
'=' is the assignment operator

```
$ awk '{print $1, $2, $3 +1.00, $4 } sundry <Ret>
  Bulbs Electrical    6.10   4
  Pen   Stationery    4.50   2
  .
  .
  .
  Keychain      Personal      4.00    1
$
```

Here the price has been increased by one rupee and the new value is displayed. We can work back to the old file by using '-' instead of '+'

```
$ awk '{ print $1, $2, $3 - 1.00 $4}' sundry   <Ret>
```

7.5.5

the "-f" option We will now put the **'awk'** commands in a file and run them. Starting with simple commands, we will go on to more complex commands. Using **'awk'** you will be able to generate various database reports.

7.5.6

files First create a file **'rep'** and enter the following awk command /stationery/{print $1, $3}

NOTE:

1. The command should not be enclosed in quotation marks

2. The word **'awk'** should not be part of the command.

3. No input file name is to be specified.

Now to run the program

```
$ awk   -f rep sundry     <Ret>
  Pens          3.50
  Pads          4.00
  Paper clips   4.00
  Pencil        0.50
$
```

The output is the same as the output we get when we type

```
$ awk '/stationery/ {print $1,$3}' sundry  <Ret>
```

The output does not look very presentablel. We will learn how to format the output a little later. But first to make the program itself look neat & readable.

```
$ cat rep                              <Ret>
/stationery/ {Print $1, $3 }
$
```

If a person were to see this program for the first time he will not understand much. Let us make the program more informative.

Step 1
Step 2
Step 3

```
/stationery/    { [The curly braces inform 'awk' that
                  there is more to come]
name =    $1      Assign $1 to 'name'
price  =  $3      Assign $3 to price
print name, price
[print $1, $3 ] close the brackets}
```

This program does not accomplish anything beyond the first version but this is definitely more readable.

In our file $4 field is taken as the **qty.** Because you have created the file you know, it is **'qty'** and not price or some tax code etc. But for a third person it does not make sense. Modify your **'rep'** program to look like this

```
/stationery/    {
        name = $1                    name is assigned $1
        qty = $4                     qty is assigned $4
    print name "quantity is" qty
  }
```

The word "quantity is" is enclosed in quotations so that 'awk' reads it as a literal and prints it as such. See the output, type

```
$ awk -f rep sundry <Ret>
  pen quantity is 25
  pads quantity is 5
  paper clips quantity is 100
  pencil quantity is 1
$
```

Extra space is to be given before enclosing the literal in quotes for better readability.

7.5.7

user defined variables: In one of the previous commands we had increased the price by one rupee. Let us assign a value to a variable **inc** and write another program to increase the price by Rs.0.75 for all the products. Create a file **"hike"**

```
{
  name = $1
  price = $3
  qty = $4
  inc = 0.75
  new price = price + inc
  print name, newprice, qty
}
```

In the above example two user defined variables were used, **'inc'** which was assigned the value 0.75. The second was "**new price**" whose value was assigned by adding the value of variable **'price'** & variable **'inc'**

NOTE
You can use the Multiplication operator (*) or the division operator (/) or subtraction operator (-). Try out similar problems by yourself. All along the output that you have been getting is not very presentable. We will now see how to format outputs. To format the output **'awk'** has borrowed the **'printf'** command from the 'C' language. We will work out an example and examine new terms or syntax as they come. Let us assume that the price of the item in the **'sundry'** file have gone up by 3.35%. Let us prepare a new list. Create a file **extra.**

```
/personal/{
            price = $3
            name = $1
            nprice = price + price * .0325
            printf "%s %s \n", name,nprice
           }
```

Let us examine this program before running it

%s → The **'s'** specifies that the characters to be printed are in the form of a string. The **%** holds or reserves the place for the string to be printed.

\n→ This tells **'printf'** to add a new line character

"%s %s \n", This means that two places must be reserved for the strings whose values are contained in the variable given after the ',' (i.e) name & nprice.

Now run this program

```
$ awk -f extra sundry          <Ret>
  Gloves 9.2925
  Keychain 3.0975
$
```

The output is exactly the same as the output that is derived from plain **'print'** statement.

7.5.8

formatting output The '%' reserves the place for the value from the variable. We have not specified how much space must be held (We should not find fault with **printf!)** Let us make corrections.

```
/personal/{
        price = $3
        name = $1
        nprice = price + price * .0325
        printf "%20s %10s \n", name,nprice
}
```

The output will be

```
Gloves      9.2925
Key chain   3.0975
```

We do not need the price in such precision. We need the price in rupees and paise only. So correct the **'printf'** statement to look like

```
printf "%20s %10.2f\n", name, nprice
```

"%10.2f" means that the total no. of character will be 10 of which two can be after the decimal. **'f'** means that it is not a string but a floating point number.

The output will now look like

```
Gloves      9.29
Keychain    3.10
```

The output in the case of the name is right justified. You can leave it like this if you want or left justify by making the following changes

```
printf "%-20s %10.2f\n", name, price
```

The output will be as follows

```
Gloves 9.29
Keychain 3.10
```

7.5.9

Redirection

It is not enough if you alone view the selected records (How selfish!). You can take a print out or store the selected records in another file. Use redirection to do so.

This is how it is done:

```
$ awk -f like sundry > > new sundry     <Ret>
$
```

Similarly awk can receive as input, the output of another process. E.g

```
$ cat /etc/passwd (:) awk '/mohan/{print $0}'
```

Does this command work ?

It will not because the field separator in the /etc/passwd file is ':' and not space. [IN SOME IMPLEMENTATIONS THIS WILL WORK WITHOUT SPECIFYING A FIELD SEPARATOR]. So what do we do? We change the field separator! Your command therefore will be

```
$ cat /etc/passwd : awk -F: '/mohan/{print $0}'
```

In the case of field separators being specified in a file there is a little difference. We will come to that after introducing another facility in **'awk'**

We have been talking of taking reports from a database and we have been getting only the field values. How about heading for the fields? Also if you want to show the total for a field then what would you do?

'awk' has got the **BEGIN & END patterns to help us.**

7.5.10

BEGIN The **BEGIN** sub-section can contain all the steps that have to be worked out before **'awk'** begins to accept and work on the input file. This section can be used to print heading or any comment lines.

7.5.11

END The **END** sub-section takes care of any statements to be appended or totals to be printed etc.

Let us try out one problem. Create a file **"bend"**.

```
BEGIN {
   print "This is a trial"
   print " NAME OPRICE NPRICE "
}
/personal/ {   name = $1o
               price = $3
               nprice = oprice * 1.25
               total = total + oprice
               ntotal = ntotal + nprice
               print name oprice nprice
          }
     END  {
                   print total ntotal
          }
```

Try this program & see

```
$ awk -f bend sundry              <Ret>
This is a trial
NAME        OPRICE   NPRICE
Gloves       9.00     11.25
Keychain     3.00      3.75
            12.00     15.00
```

{The output shown has been formatted }

Ofcourse you have to take care of formatting the output. using **'printf'**

Finally if you have to talk of change of field separator, do so in the BEGIN subsection itself

```
BEGIN {
   Fs = ":"
   }
```

In this chapter we have seen the power of the utilities like **'grep', 'sed' & 'awk'.** There is much more to this than what has been covered. But it is not in the purview of this book to cover these utilities in greater detail nor can all the other utilities be addressed here. However with some practice on what has been covered, you could easily start writing database utilities with great ease. ALL THE BEST!

EXERCISE

1. How will you insert an item record in a file ? The file is sorted on item number.
2. How will you list all files containing a given pattern ?
3. Write a script to display the argument in banner form such that the "#" is replalced by the character itself.
4. How will you print the first five lines of a file using "sed"?
5. Delete lines 5 and 8 from the file sports
6. How will you replace "all" with "everybody" in those lines which have the word twenty in the file sports.
7. Use the "sundry" file and substitute "Electrical" with "Electronic" and "Stationery" with "printing". Use only one command.
8. What is the difference between grep,fgrep and egrep?
9. While doing a substitution how will you print only the effected lines.
10. How will you print the login name, users full name, and HOME directory using awk?
11. Perform the above but in this case give appropriate headings and print the total number of users on the system.
12. How will you print the total space occupied by a file system?

8

SYSTEM ADMINISTRATION

All along you have been working in the shadow of the Superuser or the System Administrator. Your movements are restricted and you find that big brother is constantly or rather continuously monitoring your every action. Also there are a number of things that you cannot do because you are not authorised to do so. Simply put, you do not have the power that the Superuser has. But cheer up! In this chapter you will step into the shoes of the Superuser and perform all System Administration activities.

Imagine a situation where your System Administrator is indisposed (a good thing eh?) and he can't make it to the office. You call on him and he gives you the password. He cannot give you detailed instructions on the administration activities because the nurse in attendance glares at you for putting her scard under strain and chases you out. Now what? You know only the password and no more. And you have to play System Administrator!

Before we learn system administration itself, it is a good idea to know what we are going to administrate. You have to know your domain. Right?

8.1

domain

You know the number of terminals that are connected to the system and also if there are any modems connected to your system. You will also be aware of how many printers & hard disks are connected and of what capacity. Even if you do not have all the answers to the above do not worry! Recall that in chapter 2 we had discussed that all devices are treated as files and all such files are called special files. These files are in the directory **'/dev',** right ?

First thing to do is to login as super user. Type

```
login : su              <Ret>
password : xxxxxx       <Ret>
#
```

Observe that the prompt is not a $ but a # symbol. What does it mean ? It means that you have to be doubly cautious about your every move, and every command that you give. The '#' prompt is a way of reminding you that you are now in the super user mode and your power on the files/ the system is virtually limitless. You have the power to do as you like. "So watch out !". "Freedom is a restriction !"

Now change your directory to the /**dev** directory. Type

```
$ ls                         <Ret>
  console          console
  dsk 0 }
  dsk 1 }     →    disks
  dsk 10 }
  dsk 12 }
  tty 01 }
  tty 02 }    →    terminals
  tty 03 }
  tty 04 }
  lp 1 }
  lp 2 }      →    printers
  mt 1        →    tape unit
  mem         →    Memory
#
```

The above gives a list of devices connected to the system. [This list can vary and it is by no means exhaustive]

8.1.1

console Let us have a brief look at the above files first. The **'console'** file is used by the UNIX system to communicate with the console of your system [Although nowadays there is nothing like a separate 'console' on the UNIX system, the terminal that is first switched on by the super user along with the C.P.U is considered as the console].

8.1.2

dsk Now on to **'dsk'.** The listing shows **dsk0, dsk1, dsk10, dsk12,** a total of four entries. The **'dsk'** entry denotes a disk file. You are perhaps wondering how there are four disk entries when, you actually have only two disks. Well the files **dsk0** and **dsk1** are actually the 'sections' of the same disk. A hard disk is usually partitioned or divided logically into sections. The number of sections or partitions vary from installation to installation. Why this partitioning is done and why each partititon is addressed as a separate file you will soon see.

8.1.3

tty 'n' These stand for the terminals. Each **tty 'n'** represents one terminal.

8.1.4

'lp' The **lp1** & **lp2** represent the printers connected to the system. In a large installation you may have a line printer for heavy duty printing and a dot matrix printer for lighter work.

8.1.4

mt1 This is the tape drive unit which is used to take back-up.

8.1.5

mem This file refers to the memory

The terminology can be different and an installation may have more devices than that are listed here or perhaps less. But we will be refering to the list above when necessary.

You have seen the devices that are connected to the UNIX system, now we go on to the administration tasks.

Perhaps the creators of UNIX had in mind the situation you are in (i.e) you have to perform administration tasks but you do not know how. The UNIX system has its own standard procedure for start-up & shut down [Later when you have become a true System Administrator you will be able to make necessary changes].

8.2

startup When the system is switched on it runs in the single user mode and the prompt displayed is #. The only process running will be **'init'** and **swapper** and those processes that are initiated by the super user. This is because as a super user you have to ensure that the system is prepared and is free of defects before the other users can login. What are the functions to be performed before the other users can login.

→ The various file systems must be checked
→ The Date and time must be set
→ The printer spooler must be started
→ An error logging program must be started
→ The file system must be checked/monitored for usage
→ **'gettys'** to be initiated

Similarly when you move from multi-user mode to single-user mode certain processes must be terminated [Remember the **'kill'** command]

Which process to run, and which process to terminate is determined by the mode or level [run level]. Usually run level '0' is considered as single-user mode and run level '2' is considered as multi-user mode. Depending upon the level or mode the **'init'** program looks to the **/etc/inittab** file for what has to be run at this particular level. The **/etc/inittab,** has a script called **/etc/rc.**

init: The **/etc/rc** file when executed takes care of mounting the various file systems [If for example you are going to work on ORACLE then the Oracle file system will be mounted]. The printer scheduler will be started and any other program that you want executed will be initiated [We will talk of these programs by and by and also look at a sample **/etc/rc** file].

If you want to move from multi-user mode to single-user mode then type

```
$ init s <Ret>              or [ $ init 0 ]
  INIT: New run level s or [ INIT: New run level 0 ]
#
```

Now you can perform all system administration functions.

8.3

shutdown However, if you want to shutdown, UNIX provides a very orderly way out. And with good reason too! If you were to simply disconnect the system from the mains, the system will definitely be powered off but when you power on the system the next time there will be more than just big hiccups. You will be as popular as a drunk at a prayer meeting of teetotalers, as far as the other users are concerned. So you shutdown nicely. This is how you do it. First log in as 'root'. Then type

```
$ shutdown <Ret>
```

The system will ask you to confirm if you really want to shutdown. If you indicate in the affirmative, it will send a message to all the users to log off. Then it will wait for a certain grace period and then it will kill all the user processes (if any). Next it will unmount all file systems and return the system to single user mode. Now you can turn off the power supply.

You have seen how to do system start up and shut down. Now we will see how to add new users and delete users.

8.4

Add new user

The new user that you want to add has to have a HOME directory to work in. So we create a new directory which will be the HOME directory for the new user.

Recall that in Chapters 2 & 3 we had discussed how the system responds to your attempt to login. The system refers to the user's HOME directory in a file called **/etc/passwd** and also the program to be executed on login. Right ? (if you do not remember, you may as well refer the previous chapters.) Hence, as step two you have to make an addition in the **/etc/passwd** file. We will examine the **/etc/passwd** file before we proceed further.

THE PASSWD (/etc/passwd) file

Whenever a new user is created by the system administrator, or the super user, the following details have to be entered in the **/etc/passwd** file.

The password file has one entry each for every user. Each record has several fields separated by (:)

Following are the fields.

USER NAME (The name to be used at the time of login)
USER'S PASSWD - In an encrypted form (if any)
USER-ID (Each user is given a unique number by the system)
GROUP-ID (The group number of the group to which the user belongs)
USER DESCRIPTION (Usually the user's full name)
HOME DIRECTORY (The user will be placed in this directory

after logging on to the system)
The process to be executed on logging in the system as user- By default the /bin/sh is executed.

Now if Ms Sundari has joined your organisation and you have to add her name as another user under ORACLE then this is what you have to do.

i) edit the **/etc/passwd** file using any editor of your choice.
ii) Add the following line

sundari::3:1sundari ramamoorthy:/usr/oracle/sun:/bin/sh

The fields are as follows:-

sundari	:User name (login name)
::	:The password field is blank. To be given later. The UNIX system will encrypt it.
3	:User's I.D.
1	:Group I.D.
sundari ramamoorthy	:user's full name
/usr/oracle/sun	:user's HOME directory
/bin/sh	:login shell

To create a directory for Ms.Sundari

```
$ mkdir /usr/oracle/sun <Ret>
$
```

Can Ms.Sundari use this directory ? (If your answer is 'yes' then you are wrong!)

You have to change the ownership of the directory. Hand it over to Sundari.

This is how it is done

```
$ chown Sundari /usr/oracle/sun <Ret>
$
```

Now change the group too.

```
$ chgrp 1 /usr/oracle/sun <Ret>
$
```

Ms.Sundari can now login. She can give a password if she feels like.

8.5

remove user If Mr.Ramesh, your colleague has gone off to greener pastures you can remove him as an user. Delete the record that refers to him from the **/etc/passwd** file. Then remove his directory [Take a backup if required].

```
$ rm-r /usr/oracle/Ramesh <Ret>
        ( Removes files one by one)
```

8.6

General restriction So you have admitted a new user namely Ms.Sundari. Good ! Ms.Sundari in her attempt to acquaint herself with all and sundry will use all or most of the commands that you used in chapter III & IV. Ms.Sundari may be a good girl, but as the saying goes "Trust in God but tie your camel". It is a good idea to protect some of your files & directories. The protection is in the form of not giving read/write/execution privilege to the user. Some files should be made only readable and some files should be only executable files. **/etc/passwd, /unix, /etc/lc** & system directories like **/dev, /usr, /usr/lis etc.** should not be writeable. Sometimes even the disks must be non-readable.

8.7

rsh Unix provides a feature called **'rsh',** the restricted shell that can impose severe restrictions on what an user can do and what he cannot do. Your UNIX system will be used by various people in various departments. Some users tend to finish their work A.S.A.P and then they begin to explore. This can be dangerous for the system and a source of misery for you. UNIX provides you with a facility to restrict the scope of the adventerous user with the help of **'rsh'** which means restricted shell. The **rsh** helps you restrict the user from:

** changing his directory
** redirecting his output
** using commands containing '/'
** changing his PATH

The above restriction may seem very simple, yet if the user were to have only one or two directories in his PATH, he just cannot come out of them. If his directories contain some simple harmless commands like **'echo', 'date', 'cal', 'mail'** etc, his specific application program (Stores Control for example) and may be a couple of games, the user can do virtually nothing to harm the system (Unless he attacks the system with an axe! You must call the Police and say your prayers!).

8.8

password change Users generally tend to have password which are actually their initials or the names of their spouses or kids (and so forth.) With some observation and guestimate plus a small dose of luck, the password of any user can be ascertained. The usual practice is to ask the users to change their password regularly. This is easier said than done ! Users invariably forget to change their passwords after letting somebody know about it. Later if someone else plays around with their data they blame the System Administrator!.

The UNIX system comes to your rescue again. Let us examine the **/etc/passwd** file again. One of the entries is as follows

ram:k7bn OM172,E2c:5:2: mena:/usr/cae/rom:/bin/sh

Let us concentrate on the second field (i.e) 'encrypted password' field. Of course we cannot make anything out of this string of characters. But the entire string is not the encrypted password. The characters after the comma (,) have actually been inserted by the System Administrator. What do they represent ?

The first character denotes the validity of the password in weeks. The second character denotes the number of weeks after which the user can change his password. The next character denotes the number of days before which the password was last changed. This is all fine but what is the scale or standard ? What does 'M'represent and what does 'e' represent ? Does '2' mean two or something else ? O.K ! This is how you count

'.' = 0
0 = 1
1 = 2
:
9 = 11
A = 12
B = 13
:
:
Z = 36
a = 37
:
z = 63

So what does the above mean as far as the password of user 'ram' is concerned.

Let us see.

The first character after the ',' is 'E' which means that the password is valid for 16 weeks.

The second character is '2'. This means that usr 'ram' cannot change his password before 4 weeks.

Finally the third character is 'c'. This means that the password was changed 40 days ago.

By adding suitable characters after the encrypted password you can force the user to change the password regularly as desired by you. But remember that you have to add only a ',' and the first two characters. The system will take care of the rest when the user changes the password.

We have seen how the users are added or deleted by the System Administrator. To maintain effective control on the users, the responsibility of the System Administrator includes maintenance of File Systems. This means making available file systems, checking the file systems etc. The basic unit of a file system is the file itself. How is this file stored on a disk and how it is retrieved when we want to edit are some of the things you have to know.

8.9

A file system

A disk is ogically divided into blocks. The size of a block varies from 512 bytes to 4 KB. You can have block sizes of 512 bytes or 1kb or 2 kb or 4 kb. Data is read from disk or written to the disk in blocks. If you are copying a file of say 5 KB to your disk, there is no guarantee that 5 blocks of 1 KB each are available in one continuous stretch. So the data gets written on the disk, wherever there is an empty space (Unless you are over writing on existing file).

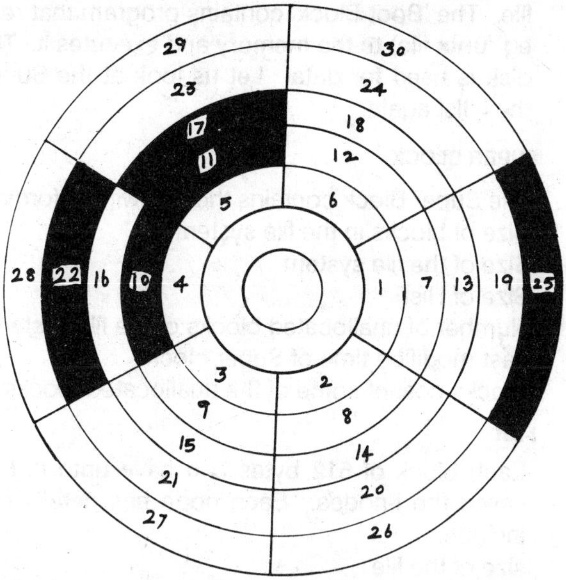

In the above figure your data could be in the blocks that are shaded (i.e.) 10, 11, 17, 22 & 25, because the other blocks in between are full.

Now how does the system know where the data is stored. Equally important is to know which is the starting point and what is the sequence in which the blocks must be read. This is an interesting problem.

If you have organised a treasure hunt or participated in one, then you would know how it is done. When you start on a treasure hunt you are given the clues to the first location or stage to be reached on your way to the treasure. The first stage will point you to the second stage and so on. The organiser of the treasure hunt will have a master list of the route the hunter(s) has to take to reach the treasure and the pointers at various stages and so forth. Let us look at something very similar in the case of a file.

The disk is divided into blocks. The location of a block on the disk is identified by an address on the block. All the blocks on the disk are not used for writing data. Details about the size of the disks, the file system present are kept in one block called the SUPER BLOCK. Another block or blocks called the 'i- list" block(s) contains details about the file. The 'Boot Block' contains program that reads a file (for eg /**unix** file) to the memory and executes it. The rest of the disk is used for data. Let us look at the Super Block and the i- list again.

8.9.1 SUPER BLOCK

The Super Block contains the following information.
Size of blocks in the file system
Size of the file system
Size of i list
Number of unallocated blocks of the file system
Last modified time of Super block
Blocks nos. of some of the unallocated blocks

8.9.2 i-list

Each block of 512 bytes can have upto 8, 64 byte nodes called the i-nodes. Each node has details of a file which include:
size of the file
type of file
owner of the file
permission of the file
address list of the file on the disk

The address list gives, in running order, the location of the file on the disk. Depending upon the order in the list, the system fetches the file asked for. The address list length depends upon the size of the file and the block size. Typically, for a large file it can have 13 entries listed. The first 10 entries point to data blocks for the data. But if the data exceeds 10 blocks then the system refers to the eleventh entry in the list which refers to a block. This block contains a list of 256 blocks which contains the data of the file.

The twelfth entry in the list goes one step further. It gives the address of a block that contains 256 block numbers and each of the 256 block numbers contain 256 block number which hold data (Are you following ?) And the thirteenth entry ? Don't worry, you can see the figure below.

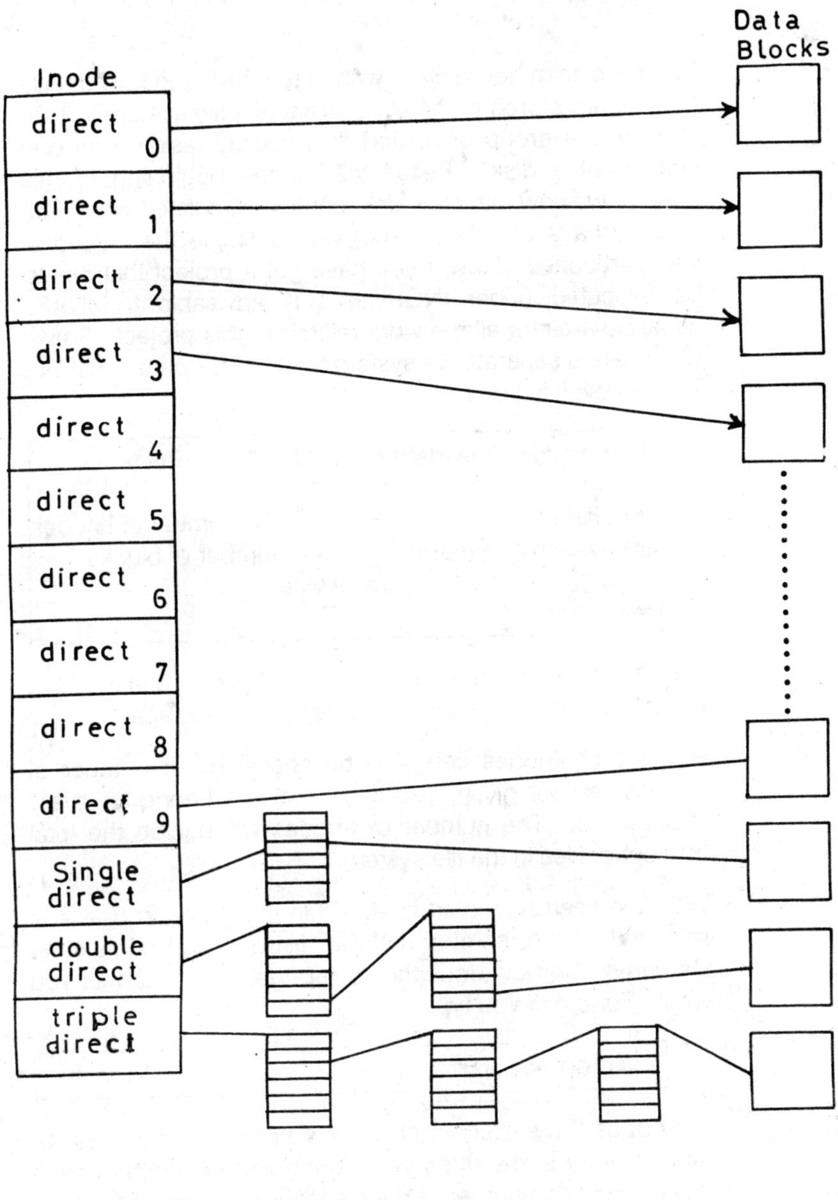

That is a lot of bytes! 17,179 MB ! This is the maximum size of a file on a disk.

Since UNIX imposes a limit that the file size should not exceed 1 MB to 2 MB we need not have to worry about a file that big.

8.10

mkfs

You have seen how a file is written to a disk and how details of a file are stored in the i-list. What is a file system? A file system is a group of related files usually residing on one section of a disk. Recall that in the beginning of this chapter we saw that four 'dsk' entries were listed when you actually have only two. That was because the hard disk was partitioned. Now if you have got a project that has to be executed under INGRES, it is advisable to allot a separate area for all the work related to this project. So we will create a separate file system for INGRES on the 'dsk11'. This is how it is done.

```
# /etc/mkfs  /dev/dsk11  20000  2500 <Ret>

the make                                  number of i-nodes
file system command                  number of blocks
                        the device
#
```

Number of blocks can be as many as the disk can hold but the size of the file system depends upon the usage.

Number of i-nodes can also be specified. If number of i-nodes are not given, you can have one i-node for every four blocks. The number of i-nodes will decide the total number of files in the file system.

We have seen how data is stored in the disk and how it is retrieved. But remember that the i-list does not contain the file name. So how does the system get to the file that you want. For e.g. if you type

```
$ vi prop  <Ret>
```

How does the system fetch the file **prop ?** The file **'prop'** has an entry in the directory. Along with this entry it also has the i- node number of the file. When the system verifies that the file is present and is readable it uses the i-node number and then fetches the file as described earlier. (This is deserved in greater detail in the chapter UNIX INTERNALS)

Now we go on to repairing the file system (if necessary). If due to some reason, the file system is corrupted or not in proper order you should first repair it and only then let the users access it. It is not practical to look through' every file system, every directory & every file to see if they are in good condition. Unix has a program to check the file system. We will go through' the process of checking/ repairing a file system using this utility.

8.11

fsck

The **'fsck'** is a 'file system checking program'. It scans the file system several times. During each pass it looks up for a particular thing. The usual things that it checks in the file system are as follows.

1. Blocks & Sizes
2. Pathnames
3. Connectivity
4. Reference counts
5. Free list

The command syntax is

```
# /etc/fsck {file system}  <Ret>
```

NOTE:

1. The prompt here is #. It means that you are in the super user mode
2. The file system name is optional. If **'fsck'** is given without arguments it will automatically pick up the file system names from the **/etc/fstab**

What follows is only a guideline, an idea as to how **'fsck'** works. Because of the criticality of this operation, it is RECOMMENDED THAT YOU READ THE USER MANUAL ON SYSTEM ADMINISTRATION SUPPLIED ALONG WITH THE UNIX O.S. SOFTWARE.

The **fsck** program will now begin to ask question that have to be answered as 'y' or 'n' for 'yes' & 'no'. It will generally ask you if it can clear a particular file, because of some defect (we will look at possible defects shortly). Since we do not know the result of our 'y' we should give 'n' as the answer to all the queries. This cautious approach is in order to see the kind of errors that exists and then see if something can be manually altered. Let us go through the motions.

```
#/etc/fsck   /usr/oracle               <Ret>
 /usr/oracle
 xx Phase 1 – checks blocks and sizes
 xx Phase 2 – checks pathname
 xx Phase 3 – checks connectivity
 xx Phase 4 – checks reference counts
 xx Phase 5 – check free list
 307 file 12514 block 9397 free
#
```

Five phases have been indicated. We will first see what is done by each phase.

8.11.1

Phase-1

A file can be retrieved or written to, only if the i-node number of the file is in order. Also the i-list should tally with the number of blocks and size of the file. Hence in the first phase the i-node data is checked for consistency. The i-list and the blocks pointed to are checked. If the i-list entry and the block pointed to, do not tally then the system throws up an error saying "BAD BLOCKS FOUND". It will continue to scan through the filesystem without waiting for any reply from you. It will also check for duplicate entries ie. the same block will be pointed at by two different i-nodes (ie two files claim the same block!). Usually the above problem occurs when the data-blocks are pointed at by the eleventh, twelfth or thirteenth entry in the i-list. These blocks are called indirect blocks, because as you know they contain address of other data-blocks. The presence of duplicate blocks is communicated to you by the system with the message "DUP". At this stage the system will prompt you with a question CLEAR?. If you answer "y" then the BAD i-nodes/blocks will be cleared [If the i-node is corrupted, take a back-up of the related file/directory and then erase the file/directory. This will free the BAD i-nodes. Later you can restore the file/directory]. But then how do you find out the filename when you are only given the i-node number? UNIX has another utility called **"ncheck"**. Note down the numbers of all the BAD i-node numbers then use the **"ncheck"** utility.

```
# /etc/ncheck -i {i-node number} {file system} <Ret>
```

This will display the filename if it is present. With the help of any editor examine the file and if it is intact take a backup and restore it later.

8.11.2

Phase-2

In the phase-2 the directory i-nodes are checked just as the file i-nodes were checked. At this stage the **'fsck'** allows you to clear the BAD i-nodes/blocks. You can however clear them later if you like. The third step deals with checking and/or establishing the links of the directories with their parent directories. Each directory in the file system being a sub- directory of another directory, the directories can be thought of as a child directory. The **fsck** program checks if the parent refered to by the child-directory's i-node is present. If the parent directory is not present then the system will ask CONNECT ?.

8.11.3

Phase-3

If you say 'y' then the system will connect this lonely directory to the **/lost+found** directory. This is very convenient method, because if a parent directory does not exist the i-node data will be considered incorrect and the system will not be able to access the file.

8.11.4

Phase-4

In Phase-4 we get back to files. Here the number of links of a file are checked. The number of links of a file represent the aliases for the same physical file. As the **'fsck'** program scans the file system it looks for the aliases and it decrements the link counter when it comes across one of the aliases. So if all the aliases are detected by the file system the count should be zero. If however that is not the case there is something wrong. There are two alternatives. 1. None of the aliases were detected by the system (possibly their parent directory does not exist, which is why they were not discovered). 2. In this case only some of the aliases were discovered.

The first situation can be got over by answering 'y' against the query "CONNECT ?" where the files are connected to the **/lost+found** directory. In the second case answer 'y' against the query "ADJUST ?". Here **fsck** will adjust the number of links depending upon the actual number of aliases found. This is the stage when you should clear all the BAD and unreferenced blocks.

8.11.5

Phase-5

Finally the phase-5 checks the free blocks list. If there are any BAD or DUP blocks the same can be salvaged by answering 'y' against the query "SALVAGE ?" Now the free blocks list is reconstructed.

"sck" exits by displaying a message "FILE SYSTEM WAS MODIFIED REBOOT !!"

Simply turn off the power, wait for a while and restart.

[/etc/mount {device name} [directory]]

8.12

mount

That was **'fsck'.** Now we will see how to mount a file system. (This is a little different from mounting a horse !). One reason for partitioning a hard disk into separate file systems is to be able to connect/disconnect (mount/ unmount) file system depending upon user requirements. For example if you have finished working with ORACLE and you want to work on say INGRES you can disconnect or unmount the ORACLE file system and mount/connect the INGRES file system. It provides for security and data integrity.

The file system to be mounted has to be mounted only on an empty directory. At the time of mounting, the directory on which the mounting is done or the mount point, will not be accessible by the other users.

/etc/mount /dev/dsk11 /usr <Ret>

The directory on which the file system has to be mounted

The device on which the file system resides.

A sample directory tree is shown below.

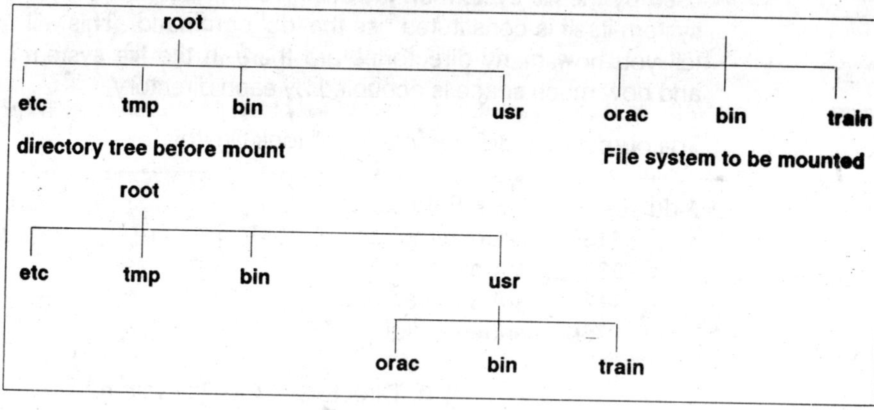

To see a display of all the file systems that are presently mounted, type

```
# /etc/mount              <Ret>
  / on / dev/dsk01        read/write on
                          Mon Dec 23 09:55:31 1991
  /usr on /dev/dsk1       read/write on
                          Mon Dec 23 09:57:39 1991
  /tmp on /dev/dskll      read/write on
                          Mon Dec 23 10:00:05 1991
#
```

8.13

df

It is not enough to get a list of the various file systems that are mounted. You would need to have more information on the disk usage, file system occupancy etc. The **'df'** command gives you information on the free blocks available and the total blocks alloted to the file system. This information will be of help for your housekeeping activities.

```
$df -t                              <Ret>
  / (/dev/dsk01)     : 4332 blocks       1092 i-nodes
              total  : 20000 blocks      2500 i-nodes
  /usr  (/dev/dskl)  : 9156 blocks       4715 i-nodes
              total  : 25000 blocks     10000 i-nodes
  /tmp  (/dev/dskll) : 13312 blocks      3672 i-nodes
              total  : 15000 blocks      3900 i-nodes
$
```

The **df** command can be given from the '$' prompt also. The **'df'** command was used to find out how much space is used by the file system on the disk. To find out how the file system itself is constituted use the 'du' command. This will tell you how many directories are there in the file system and how much space is occupied by each directory.

The output of a **'du'** command will look like this.

```
$ du /usr            <Ret>
      4136  /usr/train/mohan
      230   /usr/train/new
      1127  /usr/train/orac/one
      2766  /usr/train1/inqr
        |          |
        |          └──→ Directory in the file system.
        |
        └──→ No of bytes occupied.
```

8.14

find In chapter IV - 'Getting Started with UNIX -II' we had briefly looked up the **'find'** command. As part of your duties as System Administrator, you have to play the helpful detective. You have to find files (or even directories !) lost or misplaced by your fellow users. When we take a second look at **'find'**, you will be armed with a better magnifying glass. The standard syntax of **'find'** as you know is

```
find    [pathname]  [condition]  [action]
             |            |            └──→ Action to be performed upon success
             |            └──→ Condition for selection
             └──→ The directory or directories to search in
```

8.14a

pathname: The directory or directories in which the **'find'** should do the search. **'find'** searches recursively **through'** the directory specified.

8.14b

condition file (i.e) We have already seen the standard criteria for selecting the

-name filename
-action access time
-mtime modified time

Let us look at some other options

```
# find /usr -type f -print  <Ret>
```

Here the file 'type' is specified. The file type can be
f ordinary file
d directory file
c character special file
b block special file
So the command

```
# find /usr -type d -print  <Ret>
```

will display all directory files under the **/usr** directory

Files can also be found by specifying the user name or group name or VID/GID number. The command

```
# find /usr -user manu -print   <Ret>
```

will display all files with user name **'manu'.** If **'manu'** has an UID -5 then the command can be re-written as

```
# find /usr -usr 5 -print  <Ret>
```

If you wanted all the files of **'manu'** which have accessed more than 5 days ago then we have two conditions. In situation where you have more than one condition you must place the condition in simple braces

```
# find /usr (-usr menu -a -atime +5) -print   <Ret>
```

Will the above work ? The answer is no! Because the simple braces must be 'protected' from the shell. The correct syntax is

```
# find /usr \ ( -user menu -a -atime +5 \) -print <Ret>
```

Now about the Action part

8.14c

action **'find'** is a powerful command but it is very silent (Like the hero in a Western movie !). You have to specify the action to be performed once the files are selected. You will have observed that so far we have been using the (-print) option. The other options are

-exec [command] will execute the command on the files meeting the selection criteria

- ok [command] will execute the command on the files meeting the selection criteria but will ask you to confirm first

-cpio Refer cpio

If you want to delete all files belonging to Bobby not accessed for more than 20 days then, type

```
# find /usr\(-user Bobby -a -atime +20 \) -exec rm {} \;
#
```

NOTE

(1) The curly braces {} mean that the file meeting the selection criteria must be substituted.

(2) The third '\' is to protect the semi colon

(3) There must be a space between the '}' and the '\'.

If **-ok** is used instead of **'-exec'** it will do the same job but will ask you to confirm before deleting the file. If you type anything other than (y) for 'yes' it will skip that file and go on to the next file that is selected. Try it out yourself.

8.15

tar

"If anything can go wrong it will go wrong". This was quoted by Murphy and all of us have experienced it. Knowing this truth or the Universal law one should take precautions against accidental loss of data or a system crash. If your hard disk crashes (a good sales man will tell you that the hard disk supplied by him will not crash, but to be on the safe side you should take a back-up of your data periodically !) and if you have not taken a backup of the data you are in deep trouble. This is how you take a back-up. Most installations have a tape drive unit or if a tape drive unit does not exist a backup should be taken on floppies. The command to be used is **'tar'**.

Following is the syntax and the options

```
# tar  [c      r]   /usr   <Ret>
        |      |     |
        |      |     └──→ File system to be archived.
        |      └──→ Add this archive at the end of the existing data
        └──→ Create a new archive
```

To read back what has been archived. Use the "x" option. It **"tar"** reads the data from the tape/disk to the current directory.

```
# tar x {/bup}
         |
         └──→ The file or device is optional,
tape or a floppy disk
```

```
# tar c f    /ecc  /usr         <Ret>
      | |     |     |
      | |     |     └──→ File system to be archived.
      | |     └──→ Name of the directory
      | └──→ To device follows
      └──→ Create option
```

tar with -t option lists the various files that have been archived.

8.16 umount

We have so far seen how to mount a file system, check a file system, take a backup of a file system. We will now see how to unmount a file system. To unmount a file system you should use the **'umount'** command. But remember to give the **'sync'** command first. Before every unmounting operation and a shutdown make sure that you use **'sync'**. The **'sync'** command ensures that all the file systems in use at that time get updated. **'sync'** simply writes the information in the main memory to the appropriate files on the disk. This ensures that the information on the disk is fully updated to that point when the machine is shutdown. (If you power-off the system without using **sync** the user community will wait for you in a dark alley with some very hostile thoughts!)

A file system cannot be unmounted if it is 'busy' (ie) it is being read or written to, by any user process. Also every time you **'shutdown'** you do not have to unmount all the file systems. How to unmount?

Type

```
# /etc/umount /dev/dskll          <Ret>
```

You do not have to specify the mount point or the name of the file system to be unmounted.

8.17 cpio

'tar' is one method of taking a back-up and restoring the same. Another option available to you is **'cpio'** (copy input/output). One excellent feature of **'cpio'** is it can work in conjunction with the **'find'** command. **'cpio'** takes the list of files to be backed up from the user. It differs from **'tar'** in, that **'tar'** takes the directory name whose files are to be copied and copie the directory also as a part of the data to be backed up. It copies the entire directory structure also onto the tape. But the **'cpio'** utility copies only the files specified with the header information onto the back-up devices. If there are more than one files to be copied it writes all the files as one file on the back-up unit.

Taking a back-up : If you are backing-up all 'C' program files type

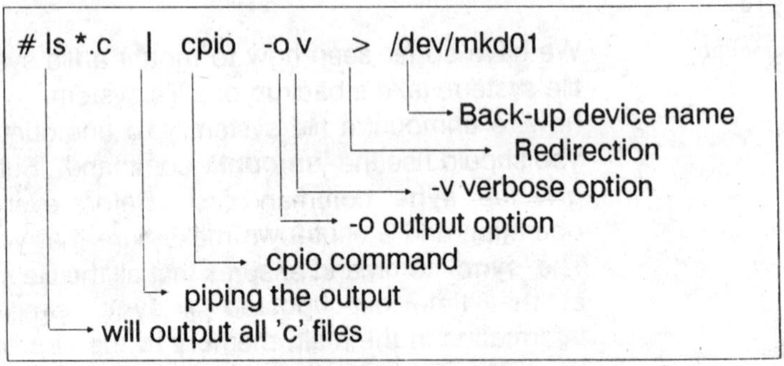

Notes

1. "-o option". The output option used for taking back-ups is one of the three options available along with the **'cpio'** command. The other options are -i and -p which we will discuss in due course.

2. The -v option will display the name of each file that is being copied onto the back-up device.

Alternatively the **'cpio'** command can be used in conjunction with, find, as follows

```
# find /usr -name *.c | cpio -ov >/dev/mkd 01
```

Finds all files in the /usr directory with the file name extension '.c'.

One advantage of **-v,** the verbose option is that the list of files backed-up can be copied onto another file for reference. This is how

```
# ls *.c | cpio -ov /dev/mkd01 1 /usr/logfile/c.prg <Ret>
```

The command may look long but it is really very simple. '1' as you know stands for standard output. So whatever is written to standard output (VDU) gets redirected to the file c.prg. Apart from posterity this file has a very useful purpose.

Suppose you are used to taking a back-up of your data & program files every week there is no sanctity in backing-up the data that you have already copied. You would like to take an incremental back-up. But a command like

```
# ls *.c | cpio -o /dev/mkd01 <Ret>
```

will copy all the **.c** files to the tape **/dev/mkd01.** This is definitely not the answer. This is what you do

```
# find /usr -newer /usr/logfile/c.prog -print | cpio -ov
  /dev/mkd01                    <Ret>
```

The **'newer'** option as you know finds all the files whose modified time is more than the modified time of the files in the /**c.prog** file. These file names are piped to the **'cpio'** command.

Since **'find'** and **'cpio'** work very well together, it was decided to do away with the **'pipe'** (Talk of bringing down barriers!!) **'cpio'** itself became an option under find. It looks like this

```
# find /usr/cee -cpio /usr/mkd01        <Ret>
```

If you want to save the list of all files copied then type

```
# find /usr/cee -cpio /usr/mkd01 -print /usr/l ogfile/
  c.prog                          <Ret>
```

In order to restore a filesystem that has been backed-up, use the **'-i'** option as the input option

```
# cpio -i /dev/mkd01              <Ret>
```

Since the files were originally copied onto the tape with the full path name they will be restored correctly to the relevant directory with their full path name.

If you are in doubt as to the exact contents of a tape use the **'- t'** option

```
# cpio -it /dev/mkd01             <Ret>
```

Since files are being restored using their full path names, the **'cpio'** will expect that all directories and subdirectories be present. To pre-empt **'cpio'** from giving you an error message use the **'-d'** option. You do not have to punish yourself by creating the various directories and subdirectories.

```
# cpio -id /mkd01                 <Ret>
```

You need to take recourse to this option if you are restoring the file system for the first time or if the existing file system has been wiped out by you.

In situation where you have a software crash or where the file system is corrupted beyond repair or where some playful soul has introduced some virus along with a games disk, you have to resort to restoring all the files. So you type

```
# cpio -ivt / < dev/mkd01
        |||
        ||└──────→ display table of contents
        |└───────→ the verbose option
        └────────→ the input option
```

Just as when we took incremental back-up, we were cautious about not recopying files already copied **'cpio'** when restoring the files is equally cautious. It checks for a match between the filenames on the system & the back-up device. If there is no match, it restores the file. If there is a match then it checks for the modification time. If the file on the system is newer than the copy on the backup device then it does not restore that particular file (a -u option will override this intelligence !).

Well that was all about backing-up and restoring files. We have seen how to create a file system, restore & back-up a file system (cpio -i & cpio -o)

What happens if one file system becomes full. You can't very well increase the size of a file system (The UNIX version described here does not have a such command). The way out is to simply create another file system (larger than the original ofcourse) and copy all the directories, subdirectories & files to the new file system.

CAUTION : Change the file system which is full and use the '.' (dot) instead of '/' with **find.**

```
# cd /usr/cee            <Ret>
```

```
# find . -print | cpio -pd /usrl/cee        <Ret>
#
```

We use '.' (dot) here because all the files will be copied using their relative path name rather than their absolute path name. This will help to be restored anywhere in the file system.

Next we will look at some sample files of **/etc/rc, shutdown** etc.

8.18

shutdown program

We had mentioned some files earlier. (i.e.) the **/etc/rc, /etc/crontab** etc. We will take a look at some of these files. Let us look at the **shutdown** file. The shutdown program in your system may run to pages. This sample program shown, is an abridged version and its purpose is to give you an idea as to how things look.

```
echo "THE SHUTDOWN PROCESS WILL BEGIN", ARE
YOU READY ?"
read ans

if [ "$ans"! = "y" -o "$ans"! = "Y" ]
  then   echo "THE SYSTEM WILL NOT BE SHUTDOWN"
         echo "DON'T USE SHUTDOWN UNLESS
                   YOU ARE READY !"
      else
      echo "THE SYSTEM WILL BE SHUTDOWN IN THE
                   NEXT  SIXTY SECONDS !
      echo "log off now, or you will lose your files" | wall
      sleep 45

      echo  "FINAL WARNING, ALL PROCESS WILL
             BE KILLED" | wall
      sleep 15
      killall
      sync
      echo  "THE FOLLOWING FILE SYSTEMS ARE
             PRESENTLY MOUNTED."
      echo  "DO YOU WANT TO UNMOUNT THEM?"
      echo  "/etc/mount"
      read x
      if [ "$x" = "y" -o "$x" = "Y"]
             then
                    umount /dev/dsk01
                    umount /dev/dsk10
                    umount /dev/dsk11
      fi
      echo "Bringing the system to single user"
      init s
      fi
```

Ofcourse you have to check if the super user is logged in as root in the root directory, if thee console is being used to run the program etc.
The next file to look at is the **/etc/rc** file. The **/etc/rc** file is invoked when we enter **'init 2'** to get into the multi-user mode. This program as you expect will mount the files that have to be mounted (if they have been unmounted during shutdown). It must initiate the **"gettys"**, the printer

scheduler, get the system date, start the **'cron'** etc. Let us write a simple program of **/etc/rc1, /etc/rc2 & /etc/rc3)**

8.19 /etc/rc file

```
if ['$2'! = "2"
        then
                echo "wrong command,syntax is "init2"
        else
                getty        run getty which opens up the
                             channel for communication with terminals.
                /etc/mount /dev/dsk10 /usr } Mount the file system
                /etc/mount /dev/dsk11 /temp)
                /etc/lib/cron Initiate the crontab program
        echo "Do you want to check the file system?"
                read ans
                if [ "$ans = "y" -0 "$ans = "y"
                        then
                                fsck
        fi
                /usr/lib/ lpschd
        echo "The following files have been mounted"
        /etc/mount
        echo "The printer has been scheduled."
        echo "You are now in the multi-user mode"
        fi
```

8.20

cron Man is dominated by the clock ! (THERE IS A TIME FOR EVERYTHING !!)

So why not get the UNIX system also to do things at desired intervals. For example:

(1) inform the users at 11.00 hrs everyday to logoff before going for their tea break. Do the same thing at lunch (i.e) 1330 hrs.

(2) Do a cleaning process every month (i.e.) delete all files that are 20 days old. (MAKE SURE THAT YOU TAKE A BACK-UP EVERY FORTNIGHT !!)

There are many more activities that you can think of. Let us see what the crontab file looks like

```
# cat/usr/tab/crontab
# min      hour   day    month  day of week  command
# (0-59)   (0-23 ) (1-31) (1-12)   (0-6)
# 0        11,13  *      *        1-6        /bin/work
  *        16     28     *        *          /bin/clean
```

The **'cron'** is a memory resident program that runs at regular intervals. It checks the file **/usr/lib/crontab** to see what has to be run at that particular time. In this case it sees that the program **/bin/work** has to be matched then it initiates the program. It also observes that the program **/bin/clean** has to be run on the 28th day of every month at 1600 hrs.

In the crontab file the
(1) first field is the minute field 0 to 59 minutes
(2) second field is the hour field 0-23 hours
(3) third field is the day field 1-31 days
(4) fourth field is the month field 0-12 months
(5) fifth field is the day of the week 0-6 sunday is day '0'
(6) sixth field is the program to be run

cron is usually used for some serious work like taking back-up, accounting system usage etc., How well **'cron'** is used depends largely on the super user.

8.21

System Accounting

Remember, that before your super user got his slipped disc, you were a mere user. You always felt that big brother was constantly watching your every move (Regular peeping Tom !). But what exactly was he monitoring ? We will go through' the 'system accounting' part of unix and then perhaps you will hold a more charitable view about your super user.

The purpose of system accounting is to keep track of the system usage, by persons and processes. The idea is to get a summary of commands used over a period. Or the usage of a system by users, branching down into number of processors , disk blocks etc. This information can be used by the super user to work out the fee to be charged if the system is being hired or to tune the performance of the system. For example if you find that some commands are used very often by an user, then the same command may be put into his home directory itself, rather than keeping those files in the end of his PATH. Alternatively, the commands not used by an user may be removed from his HOME directory, thereby giving him more work area. This results in a better overall performance of the system. How do you go about setting up an accounting system?

8.21.1

Step 1 Since somebody has to perform the system accounting function, we should create a fictitious account. It has to be called **"admin"**. In the super user mode the system does not ask for a password so the entry in the **/etc/passwd** file should have an invalid password entry. The entry in the **/etc/passwd file** should be as follows

admn:nop:4:4:Admin:/usr/adm

The HOME directory of admn should be **/usr/adm**

8.21.2

Step 2 Under the HOME directory create a subdirectory called **acct.** Under **'acct'** create three subdirectories called **nite, sum & fiscal.**

8.21.3

Step 3 Change the mode, group & owner of the directories to match the entry in the /etc/passwd file.

```
# chmod 755     /usr/adm     /usr/adm/acct/*
# chgrp 4       /usr/adm     /usr/adm/acct /usr/adm/acct/*
# chown admn    /usr/adm     /usr/adm/acct /usr/adm/acct/*
#
```

The **/usr/adm/acct/sum** directory will contain the daily accounting summary. Every time an user logs in or initiates a process, the corresponding entry is made in a file under the **'sum'** directory.

The **/usr/adm/acct/fiscal** will contain the monthly accounting summary (fiscal & monthly summary does not rhyme, does it?) The programs which manage all these functions are already available. These programs are as under

runacct: Shell script to run daily accounting

do disk: disk usage

monacct: Monthly accounting summaries are maintained

ckpacct: This program keeps an eye on **the/usr/adm/pacct** in which all system accounting entries are made. cpkacct ensures that this file does not grow too big.

8.21.4

Step 4 Since the program files are present in the **/usr/lib/acct** we must include these directories in the PATH of **'admin'**

```
PATH = /usr/lib/acct
export PATH
```

8.21.5

Step 5 The system accounting show must hit the road the moment the system moves to the multiuser mode. Hence in the **/etc/rc** file we must make this is an entry.
/bin/sk -admn -c /usr/lib/acct/start up

This is to start accounting. When we turn off the system, the system accounting should also be terminated. In the **/etc/shutdown** file add **/usr/lib/acct/shutacct**

8.21.6

Step 6 Make the necessary entries in the crontab file because these programs must be run periodically.

```
1 *    *    *  1-6   /bin/su-admn -c /usr/lib/acct/runacct
0 16   28   *  *     /bin/su-admn -c /usr/lib/acct/monacct
```

The **runacct** program will run on the 1st minute of every hour, during Mondays to Saturdays.

The **'monacct'** program will be executed at 1600 hrs on the 28th day of every month.

Well, that was system administration.

8.22

lost & found directory In phase 2 of **'fsck'** the system went about 'connecting' or linking those files who did not have a valid parent directory reference to the lost & found directory. It thrust the orphan file for adoption on the lost & found directory so that it could be accessed. You know that the constituents of the full path name have to be present if a file is to be accessed. [Pedigree in files also !!] For **'fsck'** to be successful it is a must to have a 'lost & found' directory in the root directory of every file system.

With this we will conclude this chapter. System Administration activities must be performed with a great deal of caution. Remember that you are responsible for the data and programs entered and created by the users in your organisation. And this is a big responsibility.

Let us take a quick look at the commands covered in this chapter.

shutdown	:System shutdown in an orderly manner.
init 2	:To change from single user to multi-user mode.
init s	:To change from multi-user to single user mode.
fsck	:Perform File System Check.
mkfs	:Make file systems
mount	:Connect file system specified. List File System presently mounted.
umount	:Disconnect file system specified.
df	:Report Free Blocks on the File System(s).
du	:Report disk usage by files/directories.
tar	:Tape Archiving Program for taking backups.
cpio	:"Copy Input/Output" for taking backups.
rsh	:restricted shell
find	:Locate files.

Now complete the exercise and proceed to the next chapter.

EXERCISE

1. List the devices on your system.
2. What is the main advantage of having separate file systems?
3. When and why is "sync" used?
4. What are the main commands that you will use if you are asked to write a system shutdown program?
5. What are the various phases in the "fsck" process?
6. What are the fields in the Super Block?
7. What is the difference between "cpio" and "tar"?
8. Write a shell script which will help you remove a user.

9

PROGRAM DEVELOPMENT AIDS

The shell as a programming language is good, no doubt. The same can be said of **'awk'** and other utilities. But for large applications you need a language with a larger arsenal to tackle various problems. A logical associate of UNIX is the 'C' language. Presently a large number of applications are being developed on 'C'. Unix supports other languages also like Cobol, Fortran, ADA etc., but while talking of the program development aids available with Unix, we will discuss programs written in 'C'.

This chapter will merely introduce you to some of the development aids that form part of the Unix system. You will be looking at the tip of the ice-berg. If you want to take a more detailed look at what Unix has to offer by way of program development aids. Please refer the users manual supplied with the Unix system software.

We will first look at the process of compiling the 'C' program, then we will move on to maintenance of programs developed.

9.1 Compiler

Using your favourite editor you create and edit your program. In order that the C.P.U. understands your commands, the program code must be converted into machine language. This is done by going through' a process called compilation. Compilation is done by the compiler! The compiled file is stored in another file called the executable file. You can now run the program by typing the name of the executable file as a command. If you have a program file called **Accts.c** for your accounts program you would compile it by typing

```
$ cc Accts.c        <Ret>
$
```

Since you have not mentioned any output file name, the 'C' compiler will create a file called **a.out** (Assuming that there are no errors in your source code). To run your accts.c program, you should type

```
$ a.out             <Ret>
```

However if your colleague were to compile another file by name **Mktg**.c (In your directory) then the **'a.out'** file will have as its contents, the compiled version of **Mktg.c.** So it is advisable to specify the output file name. This is how it is done.

```
$ cc Accts.c -o     Acts
$
```

Now type

```
$ Acts              <Ret>
```

to run your program.

That is very simple. Now let us take a closer look at the process of compilation. Simply stating that the compiler converts your source code into a language that the computer understands is over simplification.

A note about 'C' programs is relevant. 'C' uses 'functions' extensively. Functions are used in the construction of a 'C' program just as pre-fabricated blocks are used in the construction of buildings. All these functions need not be defined by us again and again, but are usually included in the 'C' library. The 'C' library is placed in the /lib directory and is refered by /lib/libc.a. So instead of rewriting the syntax for functions like **printf(), scanf(),** etc. We include the definition of these functions with a simple [#include "stdio.h"] statement.

We will look at a simple 'C' program. This program takes an integer input from the user and checks with the correct answer. If the number entered is equal to the number in the variable 'correct' (In this case 'correct' = 999) It prints "you have guessed correctly". Otherwise it asks you to try again.

The guess program

```
/* THE GUESSING GAME */
# include "stdio.h"
main ()
{
  int correct = 999;
  int try;
do {
printf ("Enter a number : "Enter '0' to quit\");
            try = getnum ();
            if (try = correct) {
            printf ("you have guessed correctly");
            }
   printf ("try again");
            }
            while (try ! = '0'):
}
```

Observe in the above program that we have used functions like **printf()**, **main ()** & **getnum()**. As mentioned earlier these functions need not be defined by us again. But how is the compiler to know what is meant by main() or getnum()?

The compiler is informed about these functions by the #include "stdio.h" statement. The compiler upon seeing this will know that it must refer the **'stdio.h'** file for the definition of the various functions used.

BACK TO COMPILATION !! The compiler first checks your source code for errors of syntax or if you are using variable without first declaring them etc. If everything is alright it creates an 'object' file. Next it links the object file with the library file i.e. it grafts into the object file the definitions of the functions used by you. These definitions are taken from the 'C' library. This process is called linking. The result of linking is the final executable file. It gets loaded on to the memory and is executed when the output file name is entered against the prompt. Let us look at the above one by one.

Remember that

```
$ cc Accts.c -o Acts  <Ret>
```

resulted in the final executable file called **'Acts'.**

Now if you type

```
$ cc 0c Accts.c  <Ret>
```

this will give an output **Acct.o** which is the object module.

```
$ cc -o Accts.o -o Accts
```

will now do the linking part of the compilation process.

Now why should anybody create an object file first then link it when the same thing can be done straightaway?

Frankly, the **'guess'** program is a joke! Real life application programs will be longer, much longer. With the building block philosophy of 'C', large 'C' programs are usually broken down into a number of smaller programs. The program **Accts.**c may for example be broken into **main.**c, **Arr.c**, **App.**c, **Atot.**c [WE WILL MAKE ONLY FOUR PARTS].

We can compile the four files as follows

```
$ cc main.c Arr.c App.c Atot.c -o Accts
```

If there is a syntax error in the files, say **Arr.**c and **App.**c then the linker will not link the files. However since the files **main.**c () & **Atot.**c are error free an object module for these files will be created.

Now you have to edit the files **Arr.**c & **App.**c. After editing these two files you need not recompile th files main.c () & **Atot.**c because their object module exists.

So type

```
$ cc main.o Arr.c App.c Atot.o -o Accts
```

Next when we look at **'make'** you will appreciate the idea of object files better.

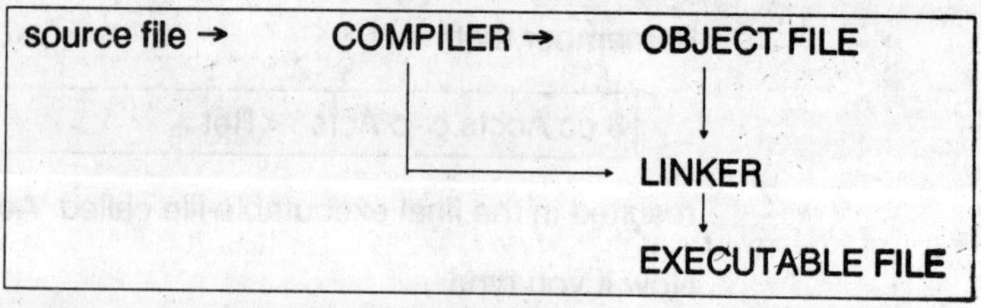

STEPS TO CONVERT SOURCE FILE TO EXECUTABLE FILE

9.2

make

While discussing the 'C' compiler we spoke of live and serious application software. More often than not there is always a change to be incorporated after 90% of the software is ready. And the change is such that it will effect atleast 70% of your program files. This means that you will have to make the appropriate changes and re-compile the files again (Perhaps this is why some of the software people go around wearing a lost expression). Let us look at the four files **main.**c, **App.**c, **Arr.**c & **Atot.**c. The **main.c** & **Atot.**c files have an include file i.e. **'spec.h'**. Now, because there are some changes in the given, specifications we have to make these changes in **spec.h.** Since the two files **main.**c and **Atot.**c depend on **spec.h**, we will have to re-compile the two files and go through' the linking process all over again. To help us out of this plight we need an utility which will

(1) record interdependencies of programs and re-compile wherever necessary.

(2) keep track of files which have been changed since the last compilation. **'make'** fits the bill. You have to inform **'make'** as to

(i) How to generate the executable file
(ii) The component files needed to generate the executable file
(iii) Dependencies of the component file.

The above details have to be given in a file usually referred to as **'makefile'** or **'Makefile'.** You can however specify your own name. Let us create a file called **Accounts**

```
$ cat >Accounts <Ret>
  # These are the steps to create the Accts program.
  Accts : main.o App.o Arr.o Atot.o
  cc main.o App.o Arr.o Atot.o -o Accts
  main.o: main.c spec.h
  App.o : App.c
  Arr.o : Arr.c
  Atot.o : Atot.c spec.h
$
```

The above file indicates the dependencies of files. Also the files to be used to generate the executable file are given. This is how you run the program

```
$ make -f Accounts
  cc -O -c main.c
  cc -O -c App.c
  cc -O -c Arr.c
  cc -O -c Atot.c
  cc main.o App.o Arr.o Atot.o -o Accts
$
```

The executable file **'Accts'** is now ready. But supposing you did not actually make any changes and wanted to use **'make'** then what happens

```
$ make -f Accts <Ret>
  'Accts' is upto date
$
```

'make' actually looks at the last modified date of all the files. If any of the files on which the target file depends on, is newer then the target file, **'make'** remakes the target file. Otherwise it takes no action. Some people would like to be doubly sure of their executable file and would like to re-compile regardless of what **'make'** has to say. If you are one of those people then this is what you do.

```
$ touch *.[ch]  <Ret>
$
```

(Now you can use **'make'**.) The **'touch'** command simply updated the modification time for all the **'.c'** & **'.h'** files.

Unix has useful remedies for some of the toothaches of programmers (even corns are treated!). Read on.

9.3

cb The 'C' program that we saw is a small program. We were able to indent the text and place the curly braces correctly. As far as readability goes, it does not look very bad either. However when constructing large programs the programmer is more concerned with the logic and control flow that he throws aesthetic to the four winds. Reading such programs can be very difficult. (Perhaps you also write your code in a similar fashion ?). To help the reader of such piece of code there is an utility called **'cb'**. This is what you do

```
$ cb games.c  games/. c <Ret>
$
```

There is one condition however that the program that goes in for the face lift must be free of syntax errors.

The untidy piece of code now looks more readable. This of course is not an universal opinion. Try it yourself once.

9.4

lint Redundancy is something very common in programming. We declare variable but do not use them. We assign wrong value to variables and get away with it because we do not use the variables. Sometimes our logic itself is not very correct. **'lint'** is used here to point out the various errors that are there in the program (It may actually be working) which if rectified will greatly improve the efficiency. The user's manual has more details on this.

9.5

cref While talking of variables, there is another situation that a programmer is faced with (i.e.) he/she does not know where a particular variable has been declared, where it is used or initialized etc. **'cref'** is an utility which creates the table containing the variables declared, the function used, the file where that function/variable are used, the function and the line number in the file. More details on this are available in the user's manual.

9.6

S.C.C.S: **Source Code Control System**

You have seen how to compile programs, how to make them more readable and also how to use **'make'.** Six months after your program **'Accts'** program was installed at the first customer location, you decide to add another feature to your **'Accts'** package. [Packages have to be more & more feature packed, whether useful or otherwise!] So you have a new version of **'Accts'.** We will call it **Accts** version 2.0. Soon another change is made and so on till you are working on version 6 of Accts! Several copies of each version of **'Accts'** have been distributed to your customers all over the country. . This is the background for what happens next.

Mr.Ramanathan who is using Accts version 2.0 has a particular problem and you have to solve it for him. If you try to simulate Mr.Ramanathan's problem on your version i.e version 6.0 it will not work. (Newer versions should not have the same bugs that are there in the older version, they can have different bugs!). The answer to this is to load the previous version (if you can remember the correct version) and go about easing your customer's ache. Every time you get a cau from a customer you have to load the relevant version and get to work. If you have been doing this, then it is not the best thing to do. Adopt **SCCS** or rather submit your files to **SCCS.**

Following is the procedure.

The **SCCS** (Source Code Control System) keeps track of changes made between version rather than keep a copy of the version itself. This is obviously to save space. Another function of SCCS is to provide a locking system so that only one person can edit a file at a time. Since **SCCS** goes by changes, it has to be able to recognize a file by certain keywords. This is how you give the keywords. At the beginning of each of the **.c** file submitted to **SCCS** add the following.

Static char sccsid[] = "%Z%%M% %I% %E%";

If you are going to submit your program to **'lint'** then change the above to read as

```
# efndef lint
        static char sccsid[] = "%Z%%M% %I% %E%";
# endif
```

The .h header files should contain

/* %Z% %M% %I% %E%";

What do these keywords stand for

%Z% is replaced by a string '@(#)'
%M% is replaced by the menu of the file
%I% is replaced by the version number
%E% is replaced by the date of creation of the latest version

A bit heavy, is it not ? Actually **SCCS** is quiet smart and can do without all this but now and then it will complain. The above exercise is to avoid giving grounds for **SCCS** to complain.

Let us see how to submit our file to **SCCS**

```
$ admin -i App.c s.App.c     <Ret>
```

Since **'admin'** can take as its input only one file at a **time** you have to give each **.c** file & **.h** file (if any) one by one.

In the above command **-i** is to inform the name of the input file to **'admin',** the output file has to be designated with **a** prefix **'s.'** (THIS IS VERY IMPORTANT).

Now let us look at the **s.App.c** file.
The lines with all the '%' signs look like this
static char sccs id[] = "@(#) App.c 1.1 9/01/92";

We will shortly see how the above is useful.

Having created the s. files (i.e. the files with the prefix s.) for all your .c files, it is advisable to get rid of the original .c files.

9.6.1

get

After submitting your files to **SCCS** you may want to compile them or perhaps edit them. When you compile a file you do not change the file, but in the second option you will be changing the file. Knowing this **'sccs'** provides you two **'get'** options. One, the plain **'get'** command which you use when you do not want to make any changes to the file. The other is the **'get -e'** option which you use when you want to edit the file.

The command [get -e s.App.c]

will place before you a **'writeable'** version of **s.App.c.** You can now make the necessary changes. However if **"get"** is used without the **'-e'** option you will only be given a version of **s.App.c** which you cannot edit. You can only view it or compile it.

9.6.2

delta Now having made your changes you have to get **sccs** to record it. You do so by using the **'delta'** command.

```
$ delta s.App.c  <Ret>
  comments? Added comment statements
  1.2
  6 inserted
  0 deleted
  37 unchanged
$
```

The **SCCS** family seem to be full of talkitive people. They talk (and complain too !) quite a lot.

Here **delta** tells us that version 1.2 has been created. It has inserted 6 lines deleted none and 37 lines have been unchanged. (If we had not added the keywords as we did earlier the **'delta'** command would have complained saying "No Keywords (cm7)". (cm7) is the error code. If you want to know what the error code stands for type

```
$ help cm7 <Ret>
```

You wil find that **sccs** is not short of words.

After creating the new version **'delta'**, deletes the older **writeable** version. You can only see the non-writeable version using the plain **'get'** option.

The other options of **sccs** are as follows:

get -r[version no] (filename)	This will get you a copy the version of the file specified.
prs (filename)	Will display the history of the sccs file specified
what (filename)	Show the versions of all component files.

Well, we have inspected the guard of honour where the program development tools are concerned. But as said earlier this is what we set out to do. If you have come so far then you must be well aquainted with UNIX by now. With this familiarity you can confidently go through the documentation supplied with the UNIX Operating System to clarify any doubts that you may have. Have fun!

10

HELLO! 'C' SHELL

While discussing the SHELL we had seen that there are a number of shells available under UNIX. And the most popular of the shells are the Bourne Shell and the C shell. So far, this book has been discussing the Bourne Shell only.

Now, we do not want to offend the creators and the users of C shell or for that matter we do not want to offend C shell itself. There is every chance that you have a C shell too on your Unix box. Frankly, by merely mentioning that the C shell is as popular as the Bourne shell we are not doing it justice. It has got some user-friendly features that even the Bourne shell does not have. So let us take a look at how the C shell is different from the Bourne shell. We will look the **"history"**, the **alias** command which the Bourne shell does not have and how the C shell treats the variables.

Prompt

The prompt for the C shell is a **"%"** instead of a **"$"** sign. However, if you are in the superuser mode, the prompt is the "#"sign regardless of the shell you are working under. So, how do we get to the C shell? Usually, when you login, you will be in the Bourne shell which means that the prompt will be a "$" sign. To go to the C shell simply type

```
$csh                <Ret>
%
```

Actually, this is like creating another subshell under your bourne shell. To find out type

```
%exit               <Ret>
$
```

There is another point to be observed that the commands given under the C shell are actually executed by your Bourne shell!! But if you insist that only the C shell should process your commands that can also be arranged. Read on.

Another way of getting into the C shell is to have your login shell changed to C shell instead of Bourne shell. You can speak to your system administrator who will do the needful. Your System Administrator will create a file called **.login** which is like your **.profile** file and another file called **.cshrsc.** In the **/etc/passwd** file your entry will be changed to read as **/bin/csh** instead of **/bin/sh.** This will put you into C shell as soon as you log in.

History

"history" is one of the unique features of the C shell. It will greatly reduce your typing effort. Let us do the necessary home work. Go back to $ prompt if you are in the C shell by typing

```
%exit           <Ret>
$
```

Create a file called **.cshrc** and enter as follows

```
$ cat> .cshrc         <Ret>
  set history =25
  alias old history
   ^D
$
```

Now go into the C shell by typing

```
$csh             <Ret>
%
```

The **.cshrc** file is read every time the C shell executes a command. In the **.cshrsc** file we have said [set history = 25]. "**history**" is an array of variable which keeps track of the commands that you enter. By making the above statement we have said that "**history**" should keep track of the last 25 commands.

Now you can continue to work as usual. Enter a couple of commands that you like. Then type

```
%history    <Ret>
  1. pwd
  2. ls - l
  3.grep sed *
  4. history
%
```

The system has actually displayed the commands that you have entered so far. When you give your twenty sixth command the first command will disappear. Now it is not enough if we merely get a list of commands entered so far. We should be able to run any of the previous commands in as simple a manner as possible. C shell has an answer to your prayers. This is what you should do.

Step 1:

```
%history    <Ret>
  1. pwd
  2. ls - l
  3. grep sed *
  4. history
  5. history
%
```

Step 2:

You can see the commands executed so far. If you want to execute the first command i.e. (pwd) then type

```
% !1        <Ret>
  pwd
  /usr/train/mohan
%
```

Next if you use **'history'** again you will find the command (pwd)is appended to the list of commands as the sixth command.

In the **.cshrc** file we had made another entry as [alias old history]. This means that we can refer to the command **'history'** by the name **'old'**. [Even commands want to travel incognito!]. Now let us look at the real advantage of the **'alias'** command.

Recall our discussions on shell functions (6.20). If you are one of those people who would still like to give MSDOS commands on a UNIX box you can do so by all means. You do not have to write shell functions. Instead simply add the following to your **.cshrc** file.

```
% vi .cshrsc                    <Ret>
  set history = 25
  alias old history
  alias dirw ls -x
  alias type cat
  alias ren mv
%
```

Now you can use the DOS commands given above instead of the Unix commands.

VARIABLES

When it comes to variables. The C shell does not believe in the concept of exporting. But as in the case of the Bourne shell the change in the value of a variable in the child shell is not conveyed to its parent shell. If you want a particular variable to be made available across **'shell'** the C shell lets you do so by defining a variable as an "environment variable". Let us first see how a variable is declared in the C shell. It is a little different when compared to variable declaration in the Bourne shell.

Regular Variables

The declaration in the Bourne shell is as follows:

```
$ name=kumar      <Ret>
$
```

Spaces between the variable and "=" and value are not permitted.

In the case of C shell it is as follows:

```
% set name = kumar   <Ret>
%
```

Spaces between the variable, "=" and the value are permitted.

To see the value of the variable, type

```
%echo $name          <Ret>
 kumar
%
```

The C shell has an interesting option where the value of a variable is a string. Let us see.

```
% set greet = (Welcome to the Unix class)   <Ret>
% echo $greet
  Welcome to the Unix class
%
```

Now if you want to see a display of only a part of the string above. It is possible. (Bourne shell does not have this facility)

```
%echo $greet [1]         <Ret>
 Welcome
%
```

In the case of the C shell when the value for a variable is a string an array is created. And you can get a display of any or all or some of the parts of the variable. Type

```
%echo $greet [1-3]          <Ret>
 Welcome to the
%
```

The above command can be entered as follows:

```
%echo $greet [-3]             <Ret>
 Welcome to the
%
```

Since the starting point has not been specified the system will display the value from the beginning to the end point specified. The reverse also holds good. Enter the following:

```
%echo $greet   [2-]             <Ret>
 to the Unix class
%
```

If you want to find the number of words in the string which has been assigned as value to a variable. Type

```
%echo $#greet          <Ret>
 5
%
```

You can also assign numeric values to variables.

```
%set num = 9           <Ret>
%echo $num             <Ret>
 9
%
```

But there is a catch here. You cannot do any manipulations on these variables. Why? Because the value in the variable is stored as a string. So the way out is assign the variable as follows:

```
% @ num1 = 10          <Ret>
%
%echo $num $num1       <Ret>
 9 10
%
```

The variable which is assigned a numeric value using "@" can be used for mathematical operations.

The Numerical Operators are as follows:

BOURNE SHELL	C SHELL	OPERATION
-lt -le	< <=	Less than, less than or equal to
-gt -ge	> >=	greater than, greater or equal to
-eq	==	Equal to
!=	!=	Not equal to
*	*	Multiplication
/	/	Divide
!	!	Logical negation
=	=~	String comparison
!=	!~	String comparison Negation

Variable Modifiers

The **"find"** command will spew out a list of names with their full path name against a command like

```
% find /usr/train -atime +2 -print    <Ret>
```

But you are not interested in knowing the full path names of the files. The C shell has some "modifiers" which will modify the final output of regular variables.

```
%set file = /usr/mohan/train/feathers.cob   <Ret>
%echo file:t
  feathers. cob
```

The "t" option knocked off the head or rather it got echo to display only the tail end. Now if you want to cut off the tail. Type:

```
%echo $file:h                        <Ret>
  /usr/mohan/train/
%
```

Since you are able to chop off any portion at will. Go a step further. There are two more options (i.e) the "e"and "r" options. Let us try them out one by one.

```
%echo $file:e                        <Ret>
  cob
%
```

Finally, the "r" option

```
%echo $file:r                        <Ret>
  feathers
%
```

Actually these options will be most useful when you want to do file maintenance. As has been mentioned earlier, the tool has been introduced to you. You have to apply it.

Before we move on to the various loops. Let us see the C shell's way of handling global or "exporting" variables.

ENVIRONMENT VARIABLES

Actually the C shell does not believe in exporting variables. It merely declares the variables as "environment" variables. Following is the syntax.

```
%setenv name = kumar        <Ret>
%csh          <Ret>    (create child shell)
%echo $ name
kumar
%
```

Please note that you cannot use the variable modifiers with environment variables.

SHELL SCRIPTS In this section we will only bring out the difference between the constructs used in the Bourne shell and the C shell. Working out examples will only be a repetition. However it is recommended that you try out the shell scripts covered in Chapter 6 using the C shell syntax for a more thorough understanding.

The REPEAT statement:

The Bourne shell has no counterpart for this statement. Following is the syntax.

[repeat n command]

```
% repeat 3 echo "Bourne has no REPEAT HA! HA!" <Ret>
   Bourne has no REPEAT HA! HA!
   Bourne has no REPEAT HA! HA!
   Bourne has no REPEAT HA! HA!
%
```

As you can see the **"repeat"** command merely repeats the commands n times. The commands given must be simple without any loops.

The **if** Loop:

There are three levels for the "**if**" loop in the "**C**" shell.

C shell	Bourne Shel
1. if (expression) command	

C shell	Bourne shell
2. if (expression) then command1 command2 endif	if control command then then commands1 commands2 fi
3. if (expression) then commands1 else if (expression) then commands2 endif	if control command then commands1 else commands2 fi
4.	if control command then commands1 elif control command then commands2 else commands3 fi

Notes:

In the case of the C shell the "if" execsutes if the expression holds good. In the case of the Bourne shell the "if" loop will function if the condtrol command is successful.

The position of the "then" clause in the two versions is different.

The "foreach"loop

C shell	Bourne Shell
foreach i * commands end	for i in* do commands done

Notes: The value for the variable "i" in the C shell can be assigned in the same way that the variable in the Bourne shell is assigned values.

The difference comes in re-directing the output. Look at the following.

Bourne shell:

```
for i in*
  do
   echo $ i
done > list
```

You can run this program and **(cat list)** will display the files in your directory. The output of the file was directed at the end of the script to a file **"list".** In the case of the C shell there is a difference. Observe the following.

C shell

```
foreach i*
  echo $i > > list
end
```

The "while" statement

C shell	**Bourne shell**
while (expression) commands end	while control command do commands done

Notes: Just as in the case of "if" the "while" loop for a C shell checks if the expression holds good. In the case of a Bourne shell construct the "while" will execute if the "control" command is successful.

The **"switch"** statement for multiple choice.

C shell	**Bourne shell**
switch (string)	case $string in
case string1.	string1)
commands:	commands
breaksw	break;;
case string 2	string2)
commands;	Commands
breaksw	break;;
default	default
commands;	commands
breaksw	break::
endsw	esac

With this we can say Good Bye to C shell. However those of you who wish to continue to work on the C shell are welcome to do so. Do not let a minor difference here and there throw you off the track. All the best!!

11

UNIX INTERNALS

Some of you who have come so far will no doubt be curious to learn more about Unix. Some will be content with what has been covered so far because they have other irons in the fire. This particular chapter is meant for the curious. The gourmand while tasting a dish will not stop with just praising the cook and taking an extra helping while ignoring the calorie counter. He would like to know how the dish was prepared, the ingredients used, the timing and seasoning and so forth. Those of you who have savored the Unix offering in the previous chapters and would like to know the inside story, read on.

The purpose of this chapter is to open the window to UNIX's Internals. We will not be going into great detail but will present you with some basics and if your interest is kindled you can refer the documentation that comes with the Operating System and some other texts that are available on this subject. But remember that this chapter leans a little towards the abstract and a little imagination will be required to fully grasp what has been described.

This chapter begins with restating Unix's features and reasons for popularity. The Unix File System will be discussed. Although some of it is a repetition it is relevant here to present a total picture. We will talk of i- nodes, directory files, buffer caches for file retrieval and so forth.

We will then look at the creation of a process. The relation between fork(), execl() and wait() system calls.

FEATURES OF UNIX

** Unix is written in "C" which makes it easy to change, add facilities to, and port it across various hardware platforms.

** A hieracheal File System which greatly enhance the ease and efficiency of file maintenance.

** Treatment of devices as files which help in increasing the ease of communication and security.

** Provision of a "shell" for each user. A user can construct an environment best suited for him/her.

** Provision of primitives like "pipe" and redirection which helps the user build complex programs from simple commands.

Some of the above statements may sound familiar. But the significance is better understood now, since you have utilized the features mentioned.

Let us go forth and take another look at the Unix File System.

First let us take a look at processes.

PROCESSES

Recall the "ps -al" command that was introduced to you in the chapter " Getting Started with Unix -I". (3.18) Let as take a look at that again.

In the explanation we saw the process status could be sleeping, or running and so forth. Let us take a closer look at the status once again.

S Sleeping:

– The process could be sleeping in the main memory.

– The process could be sleeping in the secondary storage.

O Non- Existent:

– The process is dead and has left an "exit" status.

– The process is dead but has not left an "exit" status.

W Waiting:

– The process is in the main memory and is waiting to be scheduled.

— The process is ready, but must be swapped to the main memory for the kernel to schedule it.

R Running:

— The process is executing in the kernel mode

— The process is executing in the user mode

I Intermediate:

— The process is in the transition state

Z Terminated:

— The process has been terminated.

In the chapter "Structure of Unix" you were told that the kernel creates a process table to keep track of the various processes running on the system. The kernel records the state of a process as it moves from one state to another on this process table. The process table demands more attention, so let us look at this table too. The process table will have the following details:

The Process ID.
The Users ID to determine the User's rights.
The process size.
The process status.
The signals that have to be attended to.
The location of the process in the memory or secondary storage.

Let us look at how processes execute. If you type

```
$ cat newfile
```

the kernel will initiate a process with the following algorithm.

** Check if file exists (namei())
** If so use (open()) to open the file else
** allocate free i-node from i-list
** enter file name and i-node number on directory
** free super block, i-node
** return file descriptor

Just to execute an (apparently) simple command like "cat" so many processes are involved. If each of the process is going to occupy some memory space for execution then you will have more swapping than processing!! One alternative to avoid all these problems is to limit the number of processes. But this does not solve the problem, it merely avoids it. So there must be some arrangement that will limit the space occupied by a command or an internal swapping system. And Unix has just that in the form of execl(), fork() and wait(). Before we go in and see what these processes do, let us understand what has to be done in order to appreciate the significance of these three system calls. These three musketeers work in tandem to ensure that you can have a large number of processes running with limited memory space and as little swapping as is possible.

1) If a command, say "cat" is given by the user, the space occupied by this command must be made available to the called program (Child process).

2) Since the calling command is displaced, it means that the calling program is lost and the called program or child process cannot return the result of its execution to the calling process or parent process. So we need to retain a path or an identification by means of which the child process can return the result of its execution to the parent process.

3) While the child process is executing the parent must not begin another process or continue its execution. Which means that the process must wait.

Now let us see how the three system calls operate.

execl() The execl() call replaces the original program with the called program. Only the program code is replaced, but the called program inherits the PID, the environment, the files etc. After it has completed the execution, it dies and the PID is lost. It does not know, what has to be done with the result of its activity.

The problem here is that the child process assumes the PID of the parent process and since it dies it cannot identify its parent. So there must be a way around this situation. Enter fork().

fork() As the name implies the fork() system call "forks" or duplicates the process so that the parent process retains its

PID while the child process gets a new PID. This way once the child process terminates it can still access the parent via the PID. But there is a new problem (What !)We have two identical processes. Now which of them should be run? Although both the processes are identical, the fork() call is able to identify them. It does so by returning an ID value for both the processes. For the parent process, it returns the PID of the child process and for the child process it returns 0. For a process to run, the fork() call should return a value 0. This way the twin processes situation is taken care of.

Next, when the child process is executing, the parent process should wait and collect whatever value is returned by the child. Otherwise you would end up getting bizarre results. So enter wait().

wait()

The wait() system call simply suspends the execution of the parent process till the child process returns a value. After the child terminates the parent process is allowed to continue.

This sums up the way a command is executed using the three system calls execl(), fork() and wait().

THE UNIX FILE SYSTEM

We had a brief look at the File System in the chapter on System Administration (8.9). The disk is divided into blocks. The location of a block on the disk is identified by an address on the block. All the blocks on the disk are not used for writing data. Details about the size of the disks, the file system present are kept in one block called the SUPER BLOCK. Another block or blocks called the 'I list' block(s) contains details about the file. The 'Boot Block' contains program that read a file (for eg /unix file) to the memory and executes it. The rest of the disk is used for data. Let us look at the Super Block and the I list again.

SUPER BLOCK

The Super block contains the following information.

- Size of blocks in the file system
- Size of the file system
- Size of i list
- Number of unallocated blocks of the file system
- Last modified time of Super blocks

- Blocks nos. of some of the unallocated blocks
- List of free i-nodes

The above needs no explanation.

I-Blocks

Each block of 512 bytes can have upto 8, 64 byte nodes called the i-nodes.

Each file is represented by an i-node number.It is this number that the kernel refers to while accessing the file. You will soon be introduced to the procedure of file access. We will also talk of i-node assignment to a file.

Within a file system the i-list or the list of i-nodes comes after the Super Block. If the i-node has its file-type set then it means that it has already been assigned to a file. If the file is deleted then the i-node is freed and is available for allocation to a new file. This free i-node joins the list of free i-nodes. When the kernel has to create a file it will look for a free i-node. Doing a disk read for every file creation will be very expensive in terms of time. In order to avoid this wastage of time the kernel keeps a certain number of free i-nodes in the Super Block. I-nodes are assigned from this i-list in the Super Block. Once this list becomes empty the kernel once again populates the free list.

There are two types of i-nodes.

1. The disk i-node 2.The in-core i-node.

The disk i-node:
A sample disk i-node will have the following information

i-node No.: 6371
owner: mohan
group:klass
file type:ordinary
permissions:rwxrwx--x
last accessed: Nov 10 1991 5.30 PM
last modified: Nov 10 1991 5.30 PM
i-node changed: Nov 10 1991 5.30 PM
file size:4327 bytes
links:1

disk addresses

Explanation: *** The i-node No. of the file is 6371

*** The owner of the file is mohan

*** The file belongs to the group klass

*** The file type is Ordinary (The other types of files are Directory, Special [block special/character special] and FIFO files)

*** The "owner" and the "group" have the permission to read, write and execute the file. The "others" can only execute the file.

*** It was last accessed and modified on Nov 10 1991 at 5.30 PM

*** The i-node details were changed on Nov 10 1991 at 5.30 PM If the contents of a file are changed then the i-node data also gets changed but the opposite is not true. You could for example change the ownership of the file or the permissions or the last modified time (remember "touch") but this will not change the contents of the file.]

*** The size of the file is 4327 bytes. File size is always given in bytes.

*** The number of links of this file is 1. [This i-node represents one file. Using the alias command you can have several names for the same file].

*** Finally we have the addresses on the disk where the data for this file is located.

The address list gives, in running order, the location of the file on the disk. Depending upon the order in the list, the system fetches the file asked for. The address list length depends upon the size of the file and the block size. Typically for a large file it can have 13 entries listed. The first 10 entries point to data blocks for the data. These blocks are called direct data blocks. But if the data exceeds 10 blocks then the system refers to the eleventh entry in the list which refers to a block. This block contains a list of 256 blocks which contains the data of the file. These data blocks are called in-direct data blocks.

The twelfth entry in the list goes one step further. It gives the address of a block that contain 256 block number and each of the 256 block number contain 256 block number which hold data (Are you following ?) And the thirteenth entry ? As in the chapter on System Administration we are presenting the idea as a block diagram.

What is missing is the name of the file and the contents of the file. When you enter a command [cat games] the system takes a look at the permissions data on the i-node to see if you have the permission to read this file. If you do have the permissions then it will look up the disk address list and fetch the file. If you do not have the permission then it will come back with the message [permission denied].

But when you entered the command [cat games] you did not give the i-node No., you only gave the name of the file. So how did the system get the i-node No.? One of the options of the "ls" command was [ls -i] which would list the files in the directory along with the i-node No.. So let us take a look the directory file and see what information it holds.

The Directory File

As discussed in the chapter Structure of Unix (2.3.1) a directory file can be written only by the kernel. Now do not get confused by the read/write and execute permission of a directory file. The read permission means that you can look at the contents of the directory and write permission means that you can add or delete a file from the directory.

The layout of the directory /usr/train will look like this:

Byte offset in directory	Inode Number	File Names
0	21	.
16	16	..
32	311	games
48	124	birds
64	236	feathers
80	1004	birds1
96	96	kb

Unix imposes a restriction on the length of file names. They should not be more than 14 characters long. The i-node No. occupies a two byte entry. This makes each file entry

16 bytes long. This explains the byte offset in column 1 in the above table.

The i-node No. of "dot dot" (..) is the i-node No. of the parent directory, in this case /usr and 21 is the i-node No. of the directory itself which is located at byte offset 0.

i-node assignment

Whenever a file is created the kernel makes an entry in the directory file. The kernel assigns a new i-node to the file after looking up list of free i-node available in the Super Block. Before it gets into the act of assigning an i-node it makes sure that the Super Block is not locked. Normally the kernel is able to get hold of a free i-node. However there are situations where this is not possible.

Let us take a situation where a number of jobs are submitted for execution. First, process "x" is assigned the CPU and there is a need to create a file. The kernel looks up the Super Block for free i-nodes. If there are no free i-nodes listed, the kernel searches the disk (Remember that the free i-nodes listed in the Super Block are only a part of the free i-nodes available) for free i-nodes. Having found some free i-nodes it populates the Super Block and tags the last i-node for process "x". Now process "x" goes to sleep (it has exhausted its interval perhaps) and process "y" is in the drivers seat. The process "x" has not yet copied the disk i-node into the in-core i-node which the kernel needs for its manipulations. The process "y" goes through the same process (because the Super Block has not been locked.) and ends up assigning the same i-node which was assigned to process "x". Now, when process "x" wakes up it find that the i-node 'promised' to it has got a file-type set which means that the i-node has already been assigned. When the kernel comes across this situation it once again looks up the Super Block and assigns a free i-node to process "x". By not locking the Super Block a lot of work has been duplicated. If however the Super Block had been locked by the process "x", the process "y" would have to go to sleep till the Super Block is unlocked by process "x". It would then not have to do a disk read in order to populate the Super Block with free i-nodes.

Let us take a break from i-nodes and spend some time on the kernel. Looked a functionally, the kernel can be divided in to two. One part is concerned with the file system and the other part is concerned with process control. for the moment we will look at the file system part of kernel's function.

When a user gives a command, the command actually sets into motion relevant system calls. Exactly how the various system calls work together we will see shortly. But for now just understand that for the completion of a process system calls are initiated. If there is a read/write activity, it has to do with the file system. The file system is stored on the disks or tapes. Disks or tapes are treated as special files (8.5). Since the data from disks is read in blocks and written to, in blocks disks are called block special files. The VDU and your printer are called character special files. The Unix system reads or writes to a disk via a buffer cache. Why do we need a middle-man ? Let us take Ann example. When we give a command [mv birds feathers] the following happens.

(1) The file "bird" is copied into the memory.

(2) Another file "feathers" is created (if it does not already exist). If the file exists it is opened and will be overwritten

(3) The in-memory copy of "birds" is written into the file "feathers"

(4) The file birds is deleted.

FILE RETRIEVAL We will now look at the mechanism of file retrieval and how the file name is converted into i-node numbers which the kernel will refer to for manipulations.

Assume that you have given a command as follows:

```
$ vi /usr/train/mohan
```

This is what the kernel would do.

1) It will go through the directories mentioned in the PATH to see if the "vi" command is present. If so it will proceed to the next step.

2) It recognizes the first character of the argument as "/" and it will fetch the i-node number for the "root". This will be the "working i-node".

3) Next it will check if you have the permissions to read the root directory. If so it will proceed with the next step.

4) The system reads the next word as "usr". It will do a serial search through the contents of the "root" to see if "usr" is present. If so it will go to the next step.

5) The root i-node which was used as the "working i-node" is discarded and the i-node of "usr" is now used as the "working i-node". The system then makes sure that "usr" is a directory file before doing a search for "train" and so forth till it comes to the file "mohan".

If at any iteration it comes across a mismatch then the user is told " File not found" or "permission denied".

Observe that the system makes use of the i-node number of the file/ directory when it does a search and retrieval. If instead of giving the command [vi **/usr/train/mohan**] you were to simply say [**vi mohan**] then the system will restrict the search to your current directory only. In this case the system will get the i-node number of current directory and search for a file by name "**mohan**". If the search is successful it will discard the i-node number of you current directory and adopt the i-node of "mohan" as the "working i-node". After it gets the address list of data blocks where the file "**mohan**" is stored it will retrieve the data and display it on the screen. How data is retrieved using buffers will be discussed next.

We have already seen how the kernel gets the i-node numbers to access the file. Now the file can be a large file or a small file. If the file is large,the entire file cannot be read and copied to the main memory in one stroke because of the time sharing philosophy. Since the time allotted to any process is limited, and the process has to (in this case) transfer the contents of the file from the hard-disk to the main memory in small quantums. We saw in the discussion on the use of i-nodes for file access how the kernel makes of the i-nodes. The kernel actually copies the file i-nodes into the memory. These are called in-core i-nodes. When there is a change in the file the updated in-core i-nodes are written into the file i-nodes.

Based on the information that the kernel gets from the i-nodes it begins the process of retrieving the data from the file.The system incorporates a mechanism of storing previously some of the contents from the hard disk at an intermediate spot so that the kernel does not have to go through the process of a full disk read in order to get access the next quantum of data. Assume that 10kb of data has to be transferred. Since the block size is only 1Kb the kernel can transfer only 1k at a time. The kernel therefore takes a certain amount of data and caches it for the next read operation when it comes back for the second installment of 1k. If the required data is not available in the cache then the system will do a disk read.This comes in very useful specially when programs are being executed. This cache is actually a "data buffer area" for supply of data between the hard disk and the memory. Now how is the buffer area or the cache area manipulated? Let us discuss that.

Now if the entire cache area is considered as one buffer area, it will defeat the multi-user, multi-tasking concept of UNIX. So there has to be more than one buffer area. How many there can be will depend upon the constraints of the hardware. We will assume that we have enough buffers. Each buffer will at any point of time contain data from a particular address. NO TWO BUFFERS CAN CONTAIN THE SAME DATA. In order to inform the kernel as to the data a particular buffer is holding each buffer will have a label or a header. The header of the buffer will contain details like the device number and the block number to which its data belongs. Next it has a pointer to the data area and the status of the buffer. Finally you have details of the buffer number itself which will tell the kernel as to where it belongs in the buffer pool and who its neighbors are. We will not discuss the structure of the buffer pool.

The first three are easy enough to understand but the fourth item above needs a little explanation. The status of the buffer is very important, because this will tell the kernel whether it can reassign this buffer to the next process or not. The status can be as follows:

1) Buffer is reserved for a process.

2) Buffer is full.

3) Buffer is locked/free

4) Buffer is being used by a process.

When the kernel has to do a disk read it looks into the buffer pool for a buffer very much like the way it looked for a free i-node when it had to assign an i-node to a new file. In the case of a buffer pool there are two parts. First is the free list which has free buffers in the least- recently -used order and the second is the 'hash' list which has the buffers in separate lists depending upon a device- block no combination. The kernel will look a buffer in the hash list depending upon the device and block no from which the data has to be read. We will assume for the sake of this discussion that it finds a buffer meeting its requirements. It then marks it as busy and removes it from the free list. (The situations are many. It is possible that the hash list does not contain a buffer meeting its requirements, or it finds a buffer meeting its requirements but it is locked, or that there are no buffers in the free list, or it find a buffer on the free list to marked for delayed write. What the kernel would do in these situations is interesting but it is a long story.)

Next it informs the disk driver that a buffer has been allotted for data from so and so address and then the kernel puts the process to sleep. The process will sleep till the disk driver completes the I/O and wakes up the process.

This process is now in the "ready to run" state and will wait till the kernel resumes it execution for the next step for the transfer of data from the buffer to the memory.

In the above case if the data were already in the buffer, because of a "look ahead" or "delayed write" algorithm it is so much better. The kernel is the saved the job of going through the disk read process. But how much of "looking ahead" or "delayed write " can be done will be dictated by performance constraints. If a lot of memory is allotted for buffers then the process will not have enough space for execution and a lot of swapping will have to be done.

A similar process is used when writing to the disk.

There is on item that we have not discussed in detail,(ie) the in-core i-node.

The in-core i-node is nothing but a copy of the disk i-node which the kernel uses for its manipulations. Consequently it must have more information which will be of use to the kernel. Since the i-node represents a file the in-core copy will have the logical device number of the file system to which the file belongs and the present status of the i-node. (Every body is status conscious!!) The status on the in-core copy is very critical because it tells the kernel if:

- If it is locked by another process.
- If another process is waiting for the i-node
- If the file is a mount point
- If the data on the file in memory is different from the data on the disk.
- If the in-core inode information is different from the disk i-node (due to change in ownership perhaps).

The last two points are used by the kernel if the changes made to the file or i-node data are to be saved. If so, it writes the in core copy of the file and i-node data to the disk.

This concludes the process of retrieving, writing a disk file.

We have discussed the Unix File System,file retrieval, i-node assignment, and process execution. With this let us wind up. Each of the topics discussed here actually need a lot of explanation which cannot be completed in one chapter.There are a number of books available which will discuss the above and more in greater detail. If what you have read so far has got you hooked go ahead and explore further. GOOD LUCK!

FAST TRACK

(1) COMMAND : banner

SYNTAX : banner (argument)

DESCRIPTION : displays argument in large banner format

OPTION : none

ARGUMENT : The word to be displayed as banner

(2) COMMAND : cal

SYNTAX : cal [month]year

DESCRIPTION : displays the calendar for the year or the month

OPTIONS : year -eg 1989; month - 01 - 12 for the month

ARGUMENTS : none

(3) COMMAND : cat

SYNTAX : cat filenames ...

DESCRIPTION : displays the contents of the file on the standard output (terminal)

The output can be redirected to a file using > >. If (>) is used, it appends the file1. [(cat file1 > file2)] to file2. If the filename is specified it needs data from standard input.

OPTIONS : None

ARGUMENTS : file: The name of input file(s) in the required order.

(4) COMMAND : cd

SYNTAX : cd (directory name)

DESCRIPTION : change directory: Put the user in the directory specified.

If no name is specified put the user to his HOME directory.

OPTIONS : None

ARGUMENTS : Path name of new directory.

(5) COMMAND : chgrp

SYNTAX : chgrp group filename

DESCRIPTION : Only super user can do this. Assigns the file to the new group

OPTIONS : none

ARGUMENTS : group - destination group name, filename : name of file

(6) COMMAND : chmod

SYNTAX : (1) chmod nnn filename
(2) chmod [whom] (operation, permission) filename

DESCRIPTION : changes the permission/protection bits for a file. Only owner or Super user can change the mode of a file.

OPTIONS : none

ARGUMENTS : In the first case, "nnn" are integers which can be 4 or 2 1 or the sum of any two or the sum of all three. The first "n" represents the owner permission, the second "n" is for the group & the third "n" is for others. E.g. chmod 751{filename}
In the second case "whom" is as follows.
a = all
u = user
g = group
o = others

operations can be
+ Add the permission. Do not alter other.
− Remove permission
= Add the permission, delete other permission.

The permissions can be
-r Read
-w Write
-x Execute

(7) COMMAND : chown

SYNTAX : chown [new owner] [file name]

DESCRIPTION : Changes ownership of file(s).

OPTION : None

ARGUMENTS : (1) ID of the new owner
(2) Filename whose ownership has to changed

(8) COMMAND : cmp

SYNTAX : cmp file1 file2

DESCRIPTION : Two files are compared and the byte & line no where the first difference occured is displayed.

OPTIONS : None

ARGUMENTS : file1 & file2

(9) COMMAND : comm

SYNTAX : comm [option] file1 file2

DESCRIPTION : comm compare file1 & file2 and lists the output in three columns. Col 1 has lines unique to file1, col 2 has lines unique to file2 & col 3 has lines common to both.

OPTIONS : -1 don't include col 1
-2 don't include col 2
-3 don't include col 3

ARGUMENTS : file1 & file2 to be compared.

(10)	COMMAND	:	cp
	SYNTAX	:	cp file1 file2
	DESCRIPTION	:	copying file1 to file2 or range of file to a directory. Wildcard characters can be used to specify a range.
	OPTIONS	:	None
	ARGUMENTS	:	file1 source file
	file2		destination file
	file		range of file (source)
	directory		destination directory
(11)	COMMAND	:	date
	SYNTAX	:	date [MMddhhmnyy]
	DESCRIPTION	:	date without arguments displays the system date and time. If argument is given, it sets the system date to the date and time specified.
	OPTIONS	:	None
	ARGUMENTS	:	MM : month dd : date hh : hour mn : minute yy : year
(12)	COMMAND	:	df
	SYNTAX	:	df [option] [file system]
	DESCRIPTION	:	Reports the free blocks on the file system. If no file system is specified, "df" lists the free blocks of all the file systems presently mounted.
	OPTION	:	-t. This option will also report the total blocks alloted to the file system.
	ARGUMENTS	:	Name of the file system.

(13)	COMMAND	:	du
	SYNTAX	:	du [option] [name]
	DESCRIPTION	:	Reports the space occupied in blocks by files and directories in the file system. "du" can also be used to find out the space occupied by one file or by files in one directory.
	OPTIONS	:	-a; report space occupied by each file.
	ARGUMENTS	:	File system or directory or file.
(14)	COMMAND	:	echo
	SYNTAX	:	echo [argument]
	DESCRIPTION	:	Displays the arguments or the contents of the variable which is submitted as an argument.
	OPTION	:	\n to display blank line. \c to position cursor on the same line. \t to move cursor by one tab position.
	ARGUMENTS	:	Text or variable to be displayed on the screen.
(15)	COMMAND	:	egrep (extended grep)
	SYNTAX	:	egrep [-f pattern file] filename(s)
		:	egrep x.* y.* filename
		:	egrep "A* : B*" filename(s)
	DESCRIPTION	:	searches for pattern in a file(s). Can handle multiple patterns. Can take patterns from a file.
	OPTIONS	:	-f. To read pattern from a file. "x : y" where pattern "x" or "y" is to be matched.
	ARGUMENTS	:	Name of file(s).
(16)	COMMAND	:	fgrep (fast grep)
	SYNTAX	:	fgrep [pattern] filename fgrep [-f file] filename
	DESCRIPTION	:	searches file for given pattern and can also accept patterns from a file for matching. But cannot handle regular expression.

	OPTIONS	:	same as grep.
	ARGUMENTS	:	name(s) of file(s)
(17)	COMMAND	:	find
	SYNTAX	:	find pathname {option} {action} find scans the directory specified and looks for a file that matches the option specified.
	OPTIONS	:	Multiple options can be specified. Each option to be seperated by space, preceded by "-". -atime n : The file was accessed in the last "n" days -mtime : The file was changed in the last "n" days -links n : The file has "n" links -name : The file has "name" filename -newer filename : The file looked for must be newer than the file name specified here. -print : print complete path name of files that meet these conditions. -size n: The file must have block size "n"
	ARGUMENTS	:	As above
	REMARKS	:	"n" is an integer " + n" means greater than "n" "-n" means less than "n" An "!" before the option negates the option. e.g ["! -newer" text] means not newer than file text.
(18)	COMMAND	:	fsck
	SYNTAX	:	fsck [-ny] [filesystem]
	DESCRIPTION	:	A file system check program. It checks for the correctness of Blocks and Sizes, Pathnames, Reference Counts etc, of a file system.
	OPTIONS	:	-n. This is the default option. It means that "fsck" should not attempt any repair on the file system. -y. This means the "fsck" should repair any and every damage on the file system.

ARGUMENTS : If no argument is given "fsck" performs a check on all the file systems currently mounted. Alternately you can specify the file system name whose integrity has to be checked.

(19) COMMAND : grep

SYNTAX : grep [options] string [filename]

DESCRIPTION : It is an excellent file search utility for locating a particular string. Wild cards character can also be used for string specifications.

OPTIONS : -c write only the number of lines found to the output.
-a precede each line of the output with the line number in the input file.
-r copy all lines that do not contain the string
-y ignore the case

: String: character string to search for + Wild card characters
\ Matches the following single character
^ Matches the beginning of a line
$ Matches the end of line
. Matches only single character
[] Match any of the enclosed character

ARGUMENTS : filename(s)

(20) COMMAND : head

SYNTAX : head [-n] filename

DESCRIPTION : displays the first "n" lines of the file.
By default displays the first 10 lines of the file.

OPTIONS : -n where "n" is the number of lines to be displayed.

ARGUMENTS : Name of the file(s).

(21) COMMAND : kill

SYNTAX : kill [signal number] PID

DESCRIPTION : kill terminates a process. The process is identified by process ID or PID. Usually a signal no "9" makes a sure kill.

	OPTION	:	none
	ARGUMENTS	:	PID
(22)	COMMAND	:	ls
	SYNTAX	:	ls [-option] name
	DESCRIPTION	:	lists the files in a directory or can list information specified by the option for each file.
	OPTIONS	:	-a lists all files including "." entries -i lists files with i-node numbers -l list in long form -r lists files in reverse order. -R recursive list of all files in subdirectories -t lists files sorted by last modified time -u lists files sorted by last accessed time and combination of the above + wildcard characters.
	ARGUMENTS	:	Name of file or directory.
(23)	COMMAND	:	mail
	SYNTAX	:	mail (option) mail user
	DESCRIPTION	:	An electronic mail program that allows you to send and receive messages. If mail is typed without an option, it displays message from your mail box and works in interactive mode as follows: displays next message "d" delete current message and displays the next one. S (filename) send the message to the filename "q" quits the mail program.
	OPTIONS	:	-r displays message in LIFO order -f (filename) displays message from a file other than mail box.
	ARGUMENTS	:	user: When user name is specified, the mail program accepts the text type until (Ctrl "D") is pressed. The entire text is then written to the user(s) mail box.
(24)	COMMAND	:	mesg

SYNTAX : mesg (option)

DESCRIPTION : To accord or refuse permission to others to send messages using "write".

OPTIONS : -y Allow messages
-n Refuse messages

ARGUMENTS : None

REMARKS : A super user cannot be refused permission to send messages.

(25) COMMAND : mkdir

SYNTAX : mkdir directory

DESCRIPTIONS : Makes a new directory in your current working directory.

OPTIONS : None

ARGUMENTS : Name of new directory

(26) COMMAND : mkfs

SYNTAX : mkfs [device name] [size]

DESCRIPTION : It makes a file system and reserves an amount of space on the device specified.

OPTIONS : None

ARGUMENTS : size: The size of the file system in 512 byte blocks. device name: like /dev/dsk11. Sometimes even the number of i-nodes are given. If number of i-nodes is not given, four blocks are allotted per i-node.

(27) COMMAND : more

SYNTAX : more (+line number) [+/string] file

DESCRIPTION : The file contents are displayed page by page. Once the screen is full it waits for the user to respond. If a spacebar is pressed, it displays the next screenful. If <Ret> is pressed the screen scrolls up by one line. (Ctrl "D") to page up half screen. If "n" number of integer is entered then that many lines are displayed. "more" continuously displays the percentage of file read so far.

OPTIONS : +line number. Start paging from that line number. +/string. Start paging after the first occurance of that string.

ARGUMENTS : file name

(28) COMMAND : mount

SYNTAX : mount [devicename directory] [option]

DESCRIPTION : mount connects the specified device (which is actually a file system) to the directory specified. The member files of the file system mounted become the members of the directory on which they are mounted.

"mount" without arguments and options lists the file systems presently mounted.

OPTION : -r the file system will be mounted as "read only". The default option is "r/w".

ARGUMENTS : device name: at the time eg dev/dsk011.
directory name: The directory should be empty of mounting.

(29) COMMAND : mv

SYNTAX : (1) mv file1 file2
(2) mv filename directory

DESCRIPTION : In the first option file1 is renamed as file2. In the second option the file name or range of file is moved to the destination directory retaining their original name.

OPTIONS : None

ARGUMENTS :

file1	Name of file to be moved
file2	Name of destination file
filename	Name of file(s) to be moved
directory	Destination directory

(30) COMMAND : nice

SYNTAX : nice [priority] command (Command's Arguments)

DESCRIPTION : nice is used to change the priority of a process

OPTIONS : none

ARGUMENTS : priority +n : raises priority by "n"
-n : lowers priority by "n"
where "n" is an integer

command - The name of the process for which the priority has to be changed.

Command's Argument. These are the options of the process.

(31) COMMAND : passwd

SYNTAX : passwd (username)

DESCRIPTION : used to change the log in password or to create a new password. The user need not use the argument (username). This is used only by the super user.

OPTIONS : None

ARGUMENTS : username : The name of the user whose password will be changed. Only the super user may change another user's password.

(32) COMMAND : pg

SYNTAX : pg filename

DESCRIPTION : displays contents of file(s) pagewise

OPTIONS : None

ARGUMENTS : Name of file(s).

(33) COMMAND : ":" pipe

SYNTAX : [ls] : pg

	DESCRIPTION	:	Channels the output of the left hand side command as input for the right hand side command.
	OPTIONS	:	None
	ARGUMENTS	:	None
(34)	COMMAND	:	ps
	SYNTAX	:	ps [options]
	DESCRIPTION	:	Reports every running process on the system, be it in the foreground or background. If no option is given ps reports the process initiated by the user only.
	OPTIONS	:	-a All process running in the system -l report in the long format.
	ARGUMENTS	:	none
(35)	COMMAND	:	pwd
	SYNTAX	:	pwd
	DESCRIPTION	:	Print working directory. Prints path name of current directory.
	OPTIONS	:	None
	ARGUMENTS	:	None
(36)	COMMAND	:	rm
	SYNTAX	:	rm name
	DESCRIPTION	:	Remove file from the system
	OPTIONS	:	-i verify before deleting -f delete without verification -R delete all files, lower order directories & their files.
	ARGUMENTS	:	Name of file to be deleted
(37)	COMMAND	:	rmdir
	SYNTAX	:	rmdir directory

DESCRIPTION : Remove directory or range of directories. Directories should be empty and owned by you.

OPTIONS : None

ARGUMENTS : Name(s) of directories to be removed

(38) COMMAND : sleep

SYNTAX : sleep [time]

DESCRIPTION : If a process has to be delayed by a period of time, sleep is used.

OPTIONS : none

ARGUMENTS : time in seconds

(39) COMMAND : sort

SYNTAX : sort [options] [key] (-ofile)
[-T directory] (filename)

DESCRIPTION : This option lets us sort one file or a number of files based on a key and redirect the output to an output file (ofile) which is specified or to the standard output.

OPTIONS : -f ignore case
-r reverse the sense of comparison
-n sort numeric string arithmetically
-i ignore control characters
-t 'x' where "x" is any field seperator
-b ignore leading blocks

ARGUMENTS : key: The key argument specifies the field on which sorting has to be done.

e.g. sort -t " " + 1-2 -o sortfile.
Where +1 means skip the first field & -2 means before the end of second field (i.e) the second field is the key field to be sorted

: -ofile: is the output file

-T directory: If the number of files is large, a temporary directory is opened by the name specified. If no directory is specified the system will create a direcrtory in /tmp.

: filename: The file(s) to be sorted.

(40) COMMAND : sync

SYNTAX : sync

DESCRIPTION : "sync" is like a "flush out" system. It writes all the data in the memory to the relevent file system. "sync" must be used before unmounting a file system.

OPTION : none

ARGUMENTS : none

(41) COMMAND : tail

SYNTAX : tail [options] [file name]

DESCRIPTION : displays the last "n" number of unit to as specified in the option.

OPTIONS : "n" is an integer
the units are 1 lines
b blocks
c characters

ARGUMENTS : Name of file

(42) COMMAND : tar

SYNTAX : tar (options) [file name(s)]

DESCRIPTION : "tar" stands for 'tape archiving'. It can also be used for taking back-ups on the floppy disks. "tar" with the "x" option is used to restore the backed-up data.

OPTION : -v; the verbose option, displays action taken for every file
-c; create a new archive.
-r; Add this archieve at the end of the existing data.

-t; This lists all the files on the floppy.
-f; used to specify the device name.

			-u; copy only updated files or only those files not already copied.
	ARGUMENTS	:	Name of the file(s) or directories to be archieved.
(43)	COMMAND	:	umount
	SYNTAX	:	umount [device name]
	DESCRIPTION	:	"umount" disconnects the specified device (a file system). "umount" should be used only after making sure that the particular file system is not busy. Unlike the case of "mount", you do not have to specify the mount point. Use "sync" before using "umount".
	OPTION	:	None
	ARGUMENTS	:	Device name. eg. /dev/dsk011.
(44)	COMMAND	:	uniq
	SYNTAX	:	uniq (options) [ifile] [ofile]
	DESCRIPTION	:	uniq is used to find out if any line has been duplicated. The "ifile" is the input file. The "ofile" is the output file on which you can get the text with no duplicate lines. If no "ofile" is specified, it lists the text with non repeated lines and one copy each of duplicate lines.
	OPTIONS	:	-c count duplicate lines -d display duplicate lines -u display unique lines
	ARGUMENTS	:	ifile Input file name ofile Output file name
	REMARKS	:	Sort the file before using "uniq"
(45)	COMMAND	:	wc
	SYNTAX	:	wc [-wcl] filename(s)
	DESCRIPTION	:	Performs a counting operation on the file depending upon the option specified.

	OPTION	:	-c will display the total number of characters. -w will display the total number of words. -l will display the total number of lines. will do all the above by default.
	ARGUMENTS	:	Filename(s)
(46)	COMMAND	:	who
	SYNTAX	:	who am i
	DESCRIPTION	:	lists all the users currently logged in with logged in time and terminal. "who am i" will display your name, terminal ID & login time.
	OPTION	:	None
	ARGUMENTS	:	am i
(47)	COMMAND	:	write
	SYNTAX	:	write user [tty]
	DESCRIPTION	:	A simple way to send a message to another user who is currently logged in. A (Ctrl "D") disconnects you from the receiver's terminal.
	OPTIONS	:	None
	ARGUMENTS	:	User name or tty number.

THE FINAL TEST

So you have learnt Unix! Well, the proof of the pudding is in its eating is that not so ? The questions that were put to you at the end of each chapter were to see if you have understood the concepts. If you have successfully answered all then that is OK!

But most people like to do a bit of self-evaluation to see if they are really good in whatever field they take up. For those of you who fall in this class of people there are a couple of questions. Try them out.

1. Write a shell script which will help you add a new user. The script must be interactive.

2. Write a script that will accept a value from the user and draw a Bar-Graph. You can choose your own scale.

3. Assume that you do not have the "tar" and "cpio" utilities. Write a script to take back-ups.

4. The "C" shell has the facility called "history" to record previous commands. Write a script that will emulate the same.

   (Hint: This will be a shell function.)

5. Write a shell script which will emulaate the "find" command. Unlike "find" this script must be fully interactive.